I0148854

ALLOWING
handbook

by Holly Riley

Best Selling Author of
*Allowing, A Portrait of
Forgiving and Letting
Life Love You*

Peace in Peace out® Productions
Reno, Nevada, USA

ALLOWING handbook

by Holly Riley Best Selling Author of *Allowing,*
A Portrait of Forgiving and Letting Life You

Published by Peace in Peace out® Productions

To order Allowing,
A Portrait of Forgiving and Letting Life Love you
or the Allowing Handbook contact:
www.HollyRiley.com

Library of Congress Control Number: 2012905464

Printed in the United States of America
Ist Printing - 2012

.

For my forever friend
Patricia

Thank you Thank you Thank you

My deepest joy comes with feeling my friends and loved ones wide awake to how much they matter... to the world, to every precious moment they enter, and to my heart. To my husband Patrick and my sons Travis, and Drake, it has been an honor to travel through time with you. I love who you are creating yourselves to be and feel blessed to be in your presence. Thank you for your patience, support, and never ending humor as I write and write... and write.

Dearest Patricia Rich you are my forever sister. There would be no me if there weren't a you. I appreciate your endless encouragement, foresight, and profound ability to paint reality out of dreams. Your unwavering inspiration colors my soul.

Shakti Cain, you are a light for all who come near, a steadfast reminder of what is possible! I am eternally grateful for your editing prowess and the intuitive heart that motivates your every breath.

Josephine Mason thank you my friend, for never giving up... on yourself, on me, and on life. You are a gale force wind beneath many a wing.

I love you,

Holly

Table of Contents

Spending our energy on blaming someone or something outside of us for what we are feeling often results in waiting for something outside of us to change so we can finally feel better. This can be a very long wait... a lifetime for some.

Holly Riley

The Beginning

The insights shared in the following pages were conceived during a near death experience after a long hospital stay and an inability to heal. It was a life changing interlude with many gifts, most profoundly realizing who I am beyond the thoughts I think and the body I experience through. The intricate details of dying and recovering from Crohn's disease are spelled out in my book, *Allowing, A Portrait of Forgiving and Letting Life Love You.* Here is a short version of the miracle I experienced, in hopes that you get a sense of the passionate flow of energy that surrounds you now and will forever hold us all. My journey to the invisible lovingly reminded me what I am capable of. I am certain this treasure is available for you, every moment of every day, in the very same way.

After four weeks in the hospital, being fed through a tube without gaining any weight or hope, my body shut down. After several years of battle, I was losing the fight against Crohn's disease. The end was near. The doctor informed my husband that he'd better call the family and get them to Reno if they wanted to see me again. He wasn't sure I would make it much longer as he had done everything he knew to do. My family arrived in short order from different parts of the country and let me tell you, when you look in someone's eyes for what might be the last time... you love them. Not just a little bit, completely and unconditionally. The cruel judgments and blame I had kept in place forever disappeared as I looked into their soulful eyes and caressed their aging faces. Pure gratitude filled my heart as I let their love in. It was a completion.

After everyone departed that evening, I let go of my fight to live. Peacefully, I prepared for what was next by praying, meditating, and asking whoever *Divine Intelligence* might be to please hold me close. The pain was intolerable and I was ready to go. I surrendered with all my heart. I curled up into a ball and asked for help, from anyone who might be listening.

Suddenly, softly, I was moving out of my body through the ceiling up toward the stars. The sky was dark but my path was pure light. I kept moving, gently, seeming not of my own accord. I felt tremendous peace washing through me, bathing me, and assuring me. It felt like arms of grace were holding me, whispering, *"Everything is okay."* I had never known such a feeling of serenity existed. I was floating… sound moving through me, a hum of love. It was a symphony of tones I was unfamiliar with. It vibrated filling my awareness and nurturing my soul in a way I cannot explain. Pure, calm, tranquil, complete, honor, and perfection were part of the sensation but not the entirety. I believe it was the ultimate and true potential of love, unconditional love.

My attention turned to the crumpled body below in the hospital bed as though I was nudged to look back. Immediately, I understood the roots of my illness. I became aware of the resentment I had collected and stored inside of my body. I saw the realities my blame and sorrow had etched. The thoughts were alive and taking up space in the emaciated form below. I was astounded. My unresolved past had consumed my precious body and become the ruler of my life. The 'ideas' held such cruelty I could feel the meanness of them from my new vantage point. I don't know how I understood this or exactly how to explain it but I saw the thoughts, feelings and emotions and the string of pain they harbored. Like branches of a tree they had spread into every aspect of my existence. My poor body was so tired, fragile, and broken. I was dumbfounded at how certain I had been that these hurtful ideas were a permanent part of me, a burden I was meant to carry through life.

I could NOT have been more mistaken. What I was becoming aware of while held in this sacred space was quite different from what I had always believed to be true about being human. I finally knew how I had gotten sick. It was my thoughts, they had become filters I viewed and experienced life through. Carrying my painful past forward through time had consumed my potential to heal.

With this clarity there was a new feeling being born in me, a delightful one. The more aware I became, the more thrilled I was with the idea that I was the one responsible for my reality, as strange as that may sound. This enthusiasm included a strong desire to shout my discovery out to the world so people could know how powerful they are, beyond any limiting thoughts or ideas they may be holding.

…Upon my return I was committed to become the one in charge of what I believed and experienced in life, determined to add something of value to the energetic field that embraces us all. I was ready for my new teachers to appear, and they did. My immediate studies began with Donna Hamilton, MA. MS. MFT., Robert Kirby's Inner Child work and applied kinesiology, and Harry Palmer's Avatar® Trainings on the mechanics of consciousness. Harry Palmer's profound work inspired me to become Source of my experience. I cannot imagine my life without the gifts of these teachers. They empowered me to heal on every level and I am eternally grateful for their wisdom and grace, my body fully recovered.

There is a well of appreciation in my heart for each perspective I've had the privilege of studying, The Course in Miracles, The Seth Materials, Reiki Trainings, Abraham-Hicks, The Yuen Method by Dr. Kam Yuen, Byron Katie's "The Work," Eckhart Tolle's brilliance of presence, Wayne Dyer's endless invitation to reach, Ishana Bai's Te-Energetics, Sri Amma Bhagavan's Oneness Training, Deepak Chopra, and many others who have gifted the lives of so many, inspiring us all toward Self-Realization.

Extremely thirsty, I attended every lecture or event I could on the subject of taking responsibility for where I found myself, realizing ownership was the only path to freedom. Each teacher mentioned and many unnamed will always be part of my heart... the heart I share with you.

How to Use This Handbook

The only way to move from where you are to where you want to be is to admit truthfully where you find yourself right now. This is always the place to begin.

For best results, read these pages and applications with your eyes, but be sure to feel the words with your heart. You will have little doubt to the effectiveness of the tools once applied. If an instruction or idea seems complicated or overwhelming set the book down for a while and walk away. Come back later after you have had a chance to digest and contemplate the concepts. This is not a book to read and be done with. It is a companion that will be useful in times of frustration or turmoil. It will always encourage you towards your most authentic and wise self.

Please note; these exercises are not to replace competent medical advice. If you are currently in therapy or experiencing psychosis to any degree, seek professional counseling prior to application. Please be kind to yourself on your journey. How you treat yourself is your invitation to the world... to treat you the same way.

You wouldn't have dreams unless they were absolutely possible. I am certain you can do anything you are heartily passionate about. You have the energy that creates worlds moving through you in this very moment.

CHAPTER ONE

The Invitation

The Allowing Handbook is a culmination of everything I have learned to date, written with great love for you and where you find yourself right now. I know you can manifest any success you are bold enough to desire! I believe if you decide you are ready to create a change and become the designer of your life, these pages will take you there. I am certain miracles are the norm, rather than the exception.

⌒⌒

I am realistic – I expect miracles

Wayne Dyer

⌒⌒

The invitation is for you to genuinely decide with all your heart that you are ready for a more joyful existence! DECIDE, DECIDE, DECIDE and the universe will meet you there.

Imagine, your thoughts and expectations are alive and when you give them dominion they hold court and begin constructing a reality of their own. The thoughts you hold validate the perfection of their own existence. Unknowingly we've collected and hung onto debilitating patterns of the past by over-thinking and over-analyzing, without movement toward solution. We have shut down our receivers by holding onto resentment, blame, guilt and a myriad of unhealthy criticism. It's time to open up and create some magic!

As I moved away from my body during my near death experience I became aware that my thoughts, feelings, and conclusions had designed my entire experience of reality. I had been living on automatic, reacting with all the conditioned responses of someone who felt like a victim of life with a tortured past to prove it. I was on 'protect mode' and nobody was going to get near me, unless I let them. I was having a mechanical life, intending to do just enough to gain the approval I needed from society, friends, and God, to hopefully establish salvation before crossing the finish line. I wanted someone to care about me and tell me I was doing it right, that I was living appropriately. I desperately longed for approval from someone, anyone, an imagined God most of all. The funny thing is, admiration and approval flowed in my direction often, but I never got it. Not a drop. I didn't know how to. My receiver was broken. It was impossible to fill an emptiness from the outside when it was constantly being birthed from inside.

My reality had become a predictable film. I was playing the role of projector with every image framed, colored, and coded by the perspectives I held regarding life. It was not a happy movie. Until I saw the show from a brand new viewpoint, I had no idea I had been the one holding the paintbrush of my world. I was the one coloring reality with what I believed to be true... and so was everyone else. It was my film, my paint, my decision, and my creative energy flowing in a certain direction that had designed everything I experienced. Just as you are directing your film right now.

While caressed in the arms of the nameless, I understood we are more in charge of our experience of life than we have ever believed to be true. I grasped clearly how to heal the broken form below. It was so simple, yet so beyond anything I had comprehended while living in it! I had overwhelming compassion for my body and felt very sorry for what I had caused with my stubbornness. I longed to make amends, I wanted to fix it, and somehow I knew I could. It started to make sense, thoughts were like a stream of energy and my own sorrow and non-forgiveness had poisoned me. I did it all to myself.

As I floated I became increasingly aware of the vastness I was lying in. There was an electric alive energy pulsing through me. I began to understand this current was part of who I was, I mean really was. Without the thoughts of blame and the history I had always carried forward through time. I wasn't just the body below, I was much more. My field of awareness was expansive, inclusive, and I felt serene and whole. I cherished reuniting with the truth. I was connected to everything and I was free! Sensations of trust and love filled me relative to the degree I would allow them in. It was fascinating to comprehend that it was entirely up to me how much love I permitted into my space, my awareness, and my sense of being. It was my decision. It was a lesson.

It seemed like I was swimming in grace for a very long

time, yet it was only seconds. I was there long enough to wonder, contemplate, and receive the lessons.

I was able to enjoy how the sacred energy surrounding me had been called by many names and had worn many faces. Humbly, I appreciated the perfection of humanness and how each person chooses and develops their own interpretation of this Divine Sensation, or none at all. Any choice was okay. We are all connected to 'something' beyond our individual selves and whether we choose to acknowledge it or not it remains loving, connected, and present. I delighted in comprehending how it didn't matter what we labeled it.

I also realized the name was more a product of geography, religious upbringing, or spoon feeding than anything else. Every name was absolutely perfect. I smiled having gone through a few definitions of my own. I appreciated the range of possibilities that existed for people to cling to. All the way from God, Buddha, All That Is, Cosmic God, Energy, Holy Spirit, Mohammad, Allah, Divine Mother, Divine Intelligence, The Sacred with No Name, Jesus Christ, all the way to The Matrix. It didn't mind what name you gave it, it answered to any.

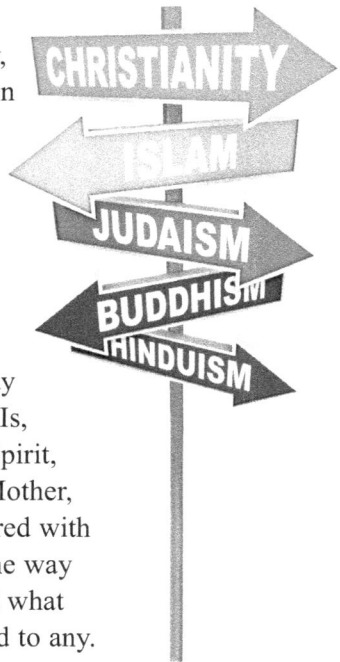

In my moment of meeting the invisible, even though I had no conscious relationship with Him, Jesus was the one holding me close and looking deeply into my eyes. I was surrounded and enveloped by his pure unwavering flow of love. It was a miracle yet it seemed perfectly normal.

I lingered, not wanting the feeling to end... the body below was part of me, but not all of me. I was bigger, wiser, all inclusive, and dearly loved. In that moment I was complete. I was exactly what and who I was meant to be. All of reality was perfect, including everyone and everything. Nothing was wrong! Everything was in the process of becoming! It was like I stepped out of a nail biting drama at the theatre and took a long deep breath of crisp fresh air and remembered the truth of whom I'd always been, of who we all are. I knew what was real... and what wasn't. It had all been a movie, a pretty scary one at times. I smiled as relief consumed me, *"I'd simply forgotten I was the director of the Holly show."* Feeling joyfully responsible I nestled in the pure pleasure of Christ's love. *I had a choice.* I HAD A CHOICE! In the stillness I felt the power of choosing, like never before.

I felt the question move through me... *"Do you want to stay or go?"*

I imagined the process of a film director, choosing the subjects, scenes, obstacles, and dreams, and the desired emotions for the cast. Deciding and planning the results, yet also allowing the creation to unfold in the making. I was motionless and quiet for what felt like a very long time, basking in the potential that I was certain held us all. I was intimately connected to the presence of Jesus, I could feel Him silently waiting for ME to choose. I felt the energy surrounding me, patiently, lovingly, and still. It was unlike anything I had ever experienced, no push, no agenda, no judgment and no attachment. I pondered, *"Do I want to go back in for the second half of the Holly show or is there another film I prefer to make?"*

It was my choice. It always had been. I understood now.

In that moment I owned my ability to decide, to decree, to declare, to direct. It was powerful, profound and mine. Deciding was a feeling I hadn't remembered so well, until then. A huge wave of recognition moved through me and something shifted in the heart of my being. I comprehended with every drop of my awareness that "I" (who we really are beyond our personality or conditioning) includes the capacity to orchestrate the next moment of existence. Each of us has the power to choose!

Consciously deciding was a monumental action for me in this moment of discovery. In this very instant the forever-ness of who I truly am, of who we all are, reached through me. I felt how we all belong to each other and how we're never acting alone and that there is an energetic field connecting everything. I sensed how we are all part of a quantum field, or grid, whether we know it or not. In this same moment I felt how every single person has access to this flow of inspiration, this potential, this love, and the ability to heal...it was palpable. I became very excited about sharing this with my family, my friends, and most of all my children. I knew what was next. My heart decided.

I returned to my broken body. The moment I made my choice, I was back in the hospital bed with tremendous gratitude for the withered form. I had another chance!

The journey from there to here is a tale of love. My body and I became friends instead of enemies. I began a life committed to honoring and respecting myself and all others. I made a decision to let go of destructive thoughts, ideas, and intentions. This commitment was the most profound decision of my life, everything changed.

I believe with all my heart that success and peace are possible for everyone.

I invite you to look deeply within yourself as you read the following pages. Perhaps like me, you have been missing the profundity of your existence... and these words will remind you.

∕≈≈

A real decision is measured by the fact that you've taken a new action. If there's no action, you haven't truly decided.

Tony Robbins

∕≈≈

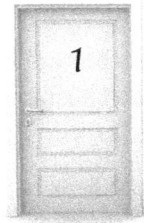

Welcome to Door #1

Choose a Feeling

•Decide what feeling(s) you prefer to have if given the choice. List them.

•Take each feeling on your list and cultivate your idea of it. Imagine it. Visualize yourself feeling it, exploring it and owning it. Experience it as deeply as possible. Soak in this feeling. Visualize breathing the sensation into your body. Do whatever it takes to cultivate your idea of this feeling. Allow the comfort of this sensation to fill your senses for one full minute.

There is no wrong way to do this, apply the steps however they work best for you.

Example 1

•David listed – feelings of satisfaction, confidence, intelligence, kindness, and importance.

•David sat quietly and recalled the feeling of satisfaction he experienced when his team reached their projected goal. He added more feeling by remembering the sense of accomplishment he had when he received his quarterly bonus. He then included the satisfaction he feels from taking care of his family, paying the bills, and doing everything he can to be sure their needs are met. He sits silently allowing this feeling of satisfaction to move through him and fill him completely for one full minute.

Example 2

•Sally listed - feeling loved, grateful, worthy, happy, generous, and organized.

•Sally closed her eyes and recalled a conversation with a dear friend when gratitude was pouring toward her. She realized she didn't really let it in and skipped over it quickly when it occurred. She decided to feel it and let it in during this exercise. She imagined her friend in front of her, became very quiet, and intended to open her heart as she recalled the words and let them soothe her. She stayed present in the feeling and allowed the sensation to fill her. It was like water pouring into her body, it saturated her senses. Once she realized how wonderful she felt she decided to let the love flow through her into her surroundings. She received her friend's gratitude and love, deeply for several minutes.

≈≈

you

Being able to direct your energy into a choice leads to every dream you have ever imagined.

YOU are the one that decides what you give your focus, energy, and conversation to. The person you've been looking for is YOU!

≈≈

CHAPTER TWO

Feelings Come From WHERE?

What do you feel when you look at this picture? Take a second and feel whatever is there. Allow without resisting. Now, describe the sensation(s) you experienced.

Did you feel sad? Compassionate? Did the photo make you want to help him, hold him, spank him, thank him?

Do you think the feeling(s) you experienced came from the picture?

If you did, you are not alone. When a room of twenty people were asked this very question they were certain the sensations they experienced while viewing this photo, came from the photo.

When asked to describe the feelings, the answers ranged from, "He isn't going to fool me" to "I felt like crying."

What each person felt was a product of their own beliefs and opinions of the picture, not a product of the photo. In this group, some were surprised that others didn't have the same reaction as they did.

We often believe our opinions are what others see when they look through their own eyes.

What you feel doesn't come from what you look at. What you feel comes from your judgment/idea about what you are looking at. What you experience when you smell, touch, hear, or observe comes from your judgment/idea of what you smell, touch, hear, or observe. What you feel comes from inside. Add your thinking to this and you can begin to see how thoughts also come with feelings. Think a thought of a child crying and what you feel is produced by your judgment/idea of a child crying. Think a thought of having the power to decide and your judgment of this idea will be what you experience.

What do you feel when you look at this picture? Take a second and feel whatever is there. Don't modify it, allow without resisting. Now, describe the sensation(s) you experienced.

If we believe that what we are feeling is a result of the world around us, we become victims of events and conditions with no hope of freedom from the pain we carry around unless, the outward event/condition somehow changes. Like Pavlov's dog, we are obliged to salivate at the ringing of the bell due to the conditioning of an external reality in our lives. Not being a dog, we have a higher potential for conscious choice. As we begin to understand that our reactions and feelings are more a choice than a circumstance, we become equipped to intuitively and powerfully make a difference in what is occurring. As we become better owners of where we find ourselves in this present moment and stop wasting energy searching for someone or something to blame, solutions and possibilities magically emerge. When a pattern is broken a new world appears.

When you understand that how you feel isn't the result of anyone or anything outside of you but rather a result of your opinion and judgment of what is occurring, your life will never be the same. Once you experience the liberation that accompanies this freedom an overwhelming sense of compassion replaces blame. You begin to recognize that suffering in others is also coming more from their own judgment, than it is from the actual predicament they're facing, just like yours. This awareness leads to an ability to transform suffering into peace. Something more fulfilling and contributory than judgment and blame become available for us to share with one another. Feelings come from inside us. With application of this knowledge to our relationships, goals, or any issue on our plate, freedom from repeating patterns becomes easier to create.

When we are no longer motivated by fear of having to experience something unfairly being imposed upon us by others and we take responsibility for our judgment, we experience palpable relief! There are no longer people making us feel a particular way! Yes, this applies to the government, employers, God, family members, ex-wives/husbands, partners, cats, dogs, etc. Can you imagine living life unafraid of what you might have to feel next as though someone else is deciding? Your life can be changed completely by the simple realization that nobody outside of you is forcing a feeling on you!

Yes, sometimes events occur that are devastating and painful and the feelings can consume us for a time. And, knowing that what we are experiencing is our judgment of the disturbing event or loss doesn't necessarily lessen the horrific pain. It does however allow us to own what we are going through inside our selves and feel what is happening instead of searching for someone to blame. Owning and allowing the pain to exist is what helps it transform and dissolve. Resisting it, blaming it, or denying it, actually makes it more consuming. This is a subject well explained in Chapter Four

In order to integrate the dreadfulness we sometimes face, we have to fully allow it to exist. As Eckhart Tolle states repeatedly in *The Power of Now*, we must focus on the feeling and direct our awareness into the location of the pain. Whether emotional or physical agony, in order for it to transform, we must be willing to be present with it and experience it. It can take a lot of effort to finally reach relief in these instances, but it can be done. However, when blame is added to our loss or misery, recovery is rarely achieved. If you've been wondering why you haven't been able to change certain situations in your life or have feelings that just don't seem to transform or go away, now you know. Likely it's because you're blaming their existence on someone or something outside of you.

Owning how we feel is the path to freedom. If you contemplate this for a moment and decide to take responsibility for your emotional state, you will experience immediate relief. If you own it, you can change it. If you blame it, someone else is in charge of how you feel.

You know what this means? Next time you're in a traffic jam and you want to blame a poor fellow driver for how you feel, well, it won't work. You'll remember whatever feeling you're having is coming from your judgment of the other driver and not from the driver's action. Ready? This is a turning point. You'll

probably begin to notice others in the traffic jam who are singing, happy, and letting life love them! More than likely, you won't be able to enjoy a good tantrum ever again. At least not without admitting and owning that the taste in your mouth is your own recipe. Truth is, you're forever and always having your own opinions for breakfast, lunch, and dinner.

Next thing you know, all those people, ideas, and events you believe are driving you crazy will become powerful reminders to let go of your criticism and take responsibility for how you are using your energy and attention. The very thing that used to annoy you will become your greatest inspiration as you use it to own your propensity to blame someone outside of you for what you are feeling. Each drop of ownership is life changing. Each incident is a golden opportunity to wake up and refocus your life energy toward manifesting dreams instead of wasting it on feeding nightmares! You'll discover that taking charge of how you spend your energy is invigorating, inspiring, and fun!

You are probably reading this because you are ready to let go of discontent and discover your ability to change certain situations and feelings in your life. You realize it is time for a new approach.

It's a good day to own what you're experiencing and open the door to new possibilities.

2

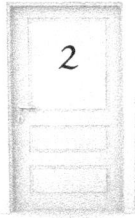

Welcome to Door #2

Own Your Feelings

•What are you experiencing that you believe is someone else's fault. Make a list.

•While looking at each item on your list identify the feeling(s) it triggers.

•Contemplate how this feeling is coming from inside of you and not from the item.

Example

David listed - unappreciated, a nasty cold, loneliness, financial insecurity, loss of my son.

David looked at the word unappreciated on his paper and immediately felt a sting of resentment toward his ex-wife and adult children for not being more grateful for all he had done for them. He continued looking at the word and realized he felt the same way about his past employer. Uncomfortable but willing, he kept exploring to see if there were any more opinions or sensations associated with his idea of being unappreciated. His father came to mind. His memory went to his childhood and how angry he used to get over his dad never appreciating him but always pointing out what was unsatisfactory. David had no idea so many thoughts were associated with not feeling appreciated. He sat quietly, observing the string of thoughts, opinions, and reactions connected to his feeling of not being appreciated.

David wondered if someone else could look at the very same word and have a completely different set of thoughts and opinions occur. He immediately thought of a friend of his that seemed to constantly receive admiration, respect, and gratitude, without effort. He looked at the word again and considered how the sensations, thoughts, and ideas that were showing up simultaneously with his focus on being unappreciated were all his. He realized what he felt was coming from inside of him. The sensations were happening in the current moment. As he continued to observe and contemplate, he had a strange and new awareness that what he was experiencing was not him but rather a string of opinions he had unconsciously adopted. He had made them important and real without investigation. He suddenly understood that he contained the ideas and that they belonged to him. They were his, but they were NOT him. He became excited and invigorated as he realized these thoughts were alive because of his own doing and not because of any person or event outside of him. He was the one feeding this line of thinking all along. David realized his feelings and thoughts were a set of responses he had learned, adopted, and considered absolute truth at one time. He realized he had a choice in the matter from this point forward.

CHAPTER THREE

Feeling Your Way to Success

Feeling isn't something we have been taught to do. For the most part it has been considered a mark of weakness and vulnerability, both professionally and culturally. Avoiding and denying feeling has frequently been rewarded by society and revered as an indication of strength.

My asking you to explore and experience some notions and feelings may seem strange and a bit like jumping the Grand Canyon without a parachute. You may believe feeling isn't your thing and perhaps it doesn't appeal to you in any regard. You may not be willing to explore. No worries, no pressure. Use the information however it works best for you. If you have the notion that feeling is for dummies I believe this chapter is exactly the thing for you! Should you decide to experiment and take a few small bites to give it a chance, I bet you will change your mind. Individuals who willingly explored found themselves reveling in unfamiliar relief.

Learning to feel and genuinely experience a sensation is an honest approach to creating and manifesting goals. This is a new method for clearing obstacles, one that has not been considered or practiced often enough. There is an intuitive and powerful part of us that comes alive as we begin to allow feelings to exist. We can become skilled in using them for dream fuel. Besides, you're a natural when it comes to feeling! You're born with this incredible ability.

Remember as a kid how you'd explore and experiment in hopes of having an exciting and exuberant experience, a FEELING? Herein lies an opportunity to have this adventure deliberately, safely, and with as much gusto as when running a football in for a touchdown or scoring a goal in soccer! You'll be astounded at how rapidly goals manifest when you decide to acknowledge and harvest your genuine feelings as fertilizer for your dreams. Guiding this unleashed power toward what we want, instead of continually and exhaustingly toward what we don't want, has proven miraculous.

A question worth considering: What would you do if you weren't afraid of anything?

Have you ever been afraid of failing? How about of your kids failing, your business failing, losing money, losing your partner, losing your health or stamina? Are you ever afraid of ending up as a nobody or wasting your life without discovering its purpose? These are fears we have all experienced.

Hear this with all your ears… it is the feeling(s) that accompany these imagined experiences that you are afraid of, not the actual event. It's the thoughts you have about the event that hurt and block you, not the actual event. These thoughts are occurring in a mental space, not in reality! Liberation is a result of recognizing the thoughts you have about an incident ARE NOT THE INCIDENT! The thoughts you are having ARE NOT YOU! They are thoughts we mistakenly believe ARE real and part of us.

You might find this funny but it is true… freedom comes with experiencing and allowing the feelings of fear we have tucked away. This way, we can finally realize these sensations or ideas cannot kill us. Every time we think of a potentially truamatic event we resist the possible pain over and over again. By repeatedly contemplating our fear of something that hasn't even happened, we increase the amount of focus and energy moving toward that idea. We actually add our creative energy to the unwanted event. The pain we are having over events that *may* occur in the future is a result of the thoughts we are thinking in the present. What a waste of our valuable energy and focus.

To fully release these fears, they must be felt. Yes your heart may beat fast, and you may sweat and squirm in discomfort for a few seconds. You may even feel like screaming, but I promise this… you will live. And, you will live no longer afraid of a certain feeling. As a matter of fact, once you allow the sensations of any reality you are fearful of to exist for a minute or two or three… you will experience independence from them. As you let go of fear and actually admit and allow the sensations, soak in them until you no longer squirm and then breathe them out, you'll have instant access to the energy that has been holding them at bay. You will be free from the thoughts that have kidnapped your joy.

Once you experience the fear you have been resisting, on purpose, because you decide to, fear of experiencing some imagined event no longer controls you! You become the owner and controller of the fear. The simplicity is scary. Feeling something on purpose gives you dominion over it. Running from a feeling means it is in charge of you. Turning around and looking what you fear in the eye is exhilarating and opens doors to reservoirs of inspiration. This is how I healed my broken body.

෬෬

All your life all you are doing is managing fear. If possible, plunge into that fear, confront the fear, and experience the fear. Only then is there hope for you to transcend fear. Take the bull by the horns.

Sri Amma Bhagavan

෬෬

Not owning or acknowledging some idea or sensation you are lugging around and trying to ignore or resist gives 'it' power over you. It haunts and grows bigger with every added thought of how it should absolutely be avoided. Thoughts and conditioning tell us it isn't rational to feel these negative or sad feelings, that it's stupid and a waste of time and energy. Thoughts tell us feeling something hurtful is wimpy stuff. Quite the contrary, not experiencing these resisted and ignored sensations can easily consume our life's energy and purpose. If we end up spending our energy resisting we don't have nearly the power to manifest or decide passionately. It takes courage to sit and just allow a sensation to exist for a couple of minutes. Particularly one we have been afraid to experience.

The interesting and important admission is that these emotions and fears are real to us, and have taken up residency as a result of our resistance. Becoming honest about who or what is taking up space in our hearts and minds will provide access to the joy and exuberance underneath. If we continue to stuff down fear, pain, anger, and blame... it will show up, eventually. Typically in the form of a physical ailment.

It's time for a new strategy.

⌒ ⌒

An uncomfortable feeling is not an enemy.

It's a gift that says, "Get honest; inquire."

We reach out for alcohol, or television, or credit cards, so we can focus out there and not have to look at the feeling.

And that's as it should be, because in our innocence we haven't known how.

So now what we can do is reach out for a paper and a pencil, write thoughts down, and investigate.

Byron Katie

Resisting something is weakening and stressful, not to mention hard on a body. Resisting and avoiding feels constrictive, it closes down our energy flow and we frequently reach for relief any way we can get it… over eating, over sleeping, hiding, over televisioning, over chocolating and many other escapes not listed. Too often we try to gain freedom by medicating ourselves and turning off all feeling. Not acknowledging or allowing a feeling in this manner is self destructive. I know about this pattern very well. I resisted pain and defeat like only a champion resister could. I tucked all my fear and sorrow way down in my body and heart so far, I didn't even know it was there. Until it almost killed me.

Try to understand this by feeling the truth of the words rather than trying to have them make sense to your mind. Turning off or avoiding feeling(s) not only builds walls against the sensations we fear, this avoidance also blocks our joy, power, and potential. Trying to be cool and not experience certain things or acting calm when we aren't has an effect on ALL categories of feelings. When we turn off feeling, we don't just turn off one aspect, we turn down the volume on all feeling. When we decide to stop acknowledging certain painful sensations, we actually stifle joyful ones as well.

When was the last time you felt a big wave of excitement, passion, or presence move through your body and soul? How about a river of exhilaration so strong adrenalin coursed through your awareness in eager anticipation? I'm not talking about sex here! I'm talking about during your normal day, while parenting, speaking to employees, having lunch, mingling with co-workers, when meeting new people on your path, when sharing ideas, possibilities, or when considering and inviting others to explore a new viewpoint. How much enjoyment do you experience in an average day of your life? Are you having fun living your life? Are you just trying to survive until it's done? What happened to that excited, adventurous, playful you? Where did the fun go? Where did YOU go? I bet if you turn your feeling back on you'll find out!

Definitions to Consider

Experience: something personally encountered, undergone, or lived through.

Synonyms of Experience: Endure, feel, have, know, pass, see, suffer, sustain, taste, undergo, witness, go through.

Merriam-Webster's Collegiate® Dictionary Tenth Edition 1993

Being willing to experience a nasty feeling for a moment beats the heck out of a lifetime of resisting it. Feeling something we have been avoiding sets free an army of locked up energy to refocus toward our goals. I have seen many people use this allowing strategy to heal a broken life and soothe a broken body. I am one of them.

≈

"Believing defines realities, and experiencing dissolves realities—that is the cycle of creation."

Harry Palmer

3

Welcome to Door #3

Use Passion as Fuel

•What feeling(s) have you been avoiding and trying not to feel? Make a list.

•Looking at each item on your list begin to recognize them as opinions and fears that you have repeatedly thought and considered real. See them as a string of ideas, opinions, or beliefs you swallowed. Consider who you would be without these thoughts. (Who would you be without this thought is a question taken from Byron Katie's book, *Loving What Is*).

•What feeling(s) would you like to feel given the choice? Make a list. While writing and experiencing your list, feel the horsepower of feeling.

Example 1

David listed – losing money in the market, not being as strong physically, dwindling business, not having the wealth I am accustomed to, getting older, boredom, insignificance to my children, insignificance to myself, uncertainty, inertia and dying.

David used the exercise in the previous chapter and immediately began to recognize the thoughts as something he was having rather than something he was. He looked at his list and felt how debilitating investing his energy and attention into these ideas has been, emotionally and physically. Just looking at them was exhausting for him. He grasped how he'd been giving his focus to these ideas unconsciously and for a very long time. As he reviewed the list he had an insight, each item was related to a feeling of being inadequate. He imagined what it would be like to no longer have this thought or worry in his life. He knew he would be more confident, capable and adequate without this thought. He felt an inkling of what life could be like and realized once again, he was not the thoughts but the holder of them.

David's preferences – Satisfied, genuinely happy for the success of others, strong, trusting of the future, important, valuable, and respected. He noticed as he wrote that he sat up a little straighter and felt some degree of relief. He was starting to understand the power of a thought.

Example 2

Sally's list of avoided feelings – not mattering to my family, not mattering in general, feeling stupid, being unworthy, being judged by others, feeling the doubt I hide, chronic worry about my daughter, isolation, failure, feeling selfish, that life could be meaningless, that I have no purpose.

Sally became discouraged and even a little angry when she looked at her list. She felt she had worked on all of these issues before and was frustrated with the fact that she has written them down yet again. She began beating herself up and making herself very wrong with a conversation of being stupid, unworthy, and a failure. She wondered if anything would ever change and wanted to quit exploring. She took a deep breath and relaxed for a minute and noticed the question, "Who would you be without this thought," and she laughed out loud. Her answer was, "I would be free." She felt it for a second and got it. "These are all thoughts and I can choose to have them or not." She liked imagining her life without them! She contemplated who she would be, what she would feel, and how she would relate to her family and friends and she smiled.

Sally's feelings of choice – I want to be more in charge of how I feel. More deliberate, aware of my thoughts, present, real, loving, kind to myself, honoring of myself, more able to fill my own cup instead of wanting others to do it, honest and in love with life. She felt very satisfied with her list and silently made a promise to pay more attention to the ideas she entertains with her energy.

CHAPTER FOUR

Catch & Release

This is a simple process that works on anything, everywhere, all the time, no matter what. Individuals have become so efficient with the steps they've been able to produce results in seconds. You can apply this strategy to absolutely every obstacle or difficulty you are experiencing in life... or will ever experience in life and it will always bring relief and more peace. Catch & Release will empower you to manage and let go of feelings, ideas, or sensations you prefer not to have and replace them with feelings, ideas, and sensations of choice. With a little practice it becomes an important tool to keep in your pocket.

The first step is to CATCH when you begin having a feeling, idea, or sensation you don't like. Notice it. Catch yourself as you begin to close up, get frustrated, or start resisting something. Notice when you start to become emotional, want to shut down, or rip someone's head off. Notice when you begin to feel bad or frustrated. Catch means to pay attention to your attitude, your feelings, your vibration and notice when you begin a downward spiral. It's that basic. Catch it as quickly as you can. If you realize later when the frustration started, no worries, you can go back to it and the process still works. Catching yourself is the first step in claiming the energy and attention you have been using to oppose life so you can redirect your efforts toward designing a life you love to live.

Helpful hints... become aware of any destructive response you may have when faced with a situation, person, or circumstance that typically disturbs you (yes, this person may be you). Catching yourself when you begin to feel a shift from comfortable to uncomfortable, from feeling good to feeling bad, from feeling connected to experiencing alienation, is a big step toward transformation. These reactions are indications of the luggage (pain and patterns) we are carrying through life. Being able to recognize how you behave when you are faced with a feeling you don't want to have is a monumental achievement. This is an opportunity to create significant change. Good Catch! It's a powerful intention to become self aware when you start to resist something.

I find it revealing to Catch any propensity I have to criticize (criticism is resistance). Also, if I go to open the refrigerator when I am NOT hungry, I ask myself, *"What am I resisting feeling right now?"* It's usually regarding 'being controlled' or 'following rules.' Anytime I feel resentful it's a signal I am avoiding feeling or owning something.

Welcome to the Catch program. It requires paying attention to how you are feeling so you can be in charge of it, instead of it being in charge of you.

≈≈

One of the curious things about this universe is that if you create something and you're not willing to experience it, you keep right on creating it. It will wait for you! However long it takes!

Harry Palmer

The Release aspect includes discovering the feeling you're creating and holding inside but are avoiding. This step allows you to finally own it so you can release it and feel better. This Release step includes choosing how you want to feel. This all flows into one smooth action after a few applications. Releasing begins by asking yourself what feeling, sensation or idea you are trying NOT to experience as you begin to feel badly. When you Catch yourself closing down or feeling perplexed, investigate by asking, "What feeling am I avoiding experiencing right now? What sensation or idea am I pushing against?" This is a miraculous question because it guides you right to the feeling, idea, or sensation you have been unconsciously creating and spending energy resisting, often for much of your existence. Once you've discovered the idea or sensation you're denying you can look it in the eye and become free of it. Remember feelings come from inside. We are the maker of them and if we avoid them they consume our life force. Catch & Release is an easy method of collecting creative energy.

Don't worry about the WHO, WHAT, and WHY of the sensation, feeling, or idea you Catch. Don't spend much time dissecting whether you have the right one or not. If you try and figure out where the feeling came from (i.e. fell on your head as a child) or who is to blame for it, you can easily get lost in thinking. Let it be easy, the feeling you are resisting is right there, in the moment you pulled away or became upset. Go back in time to the experience and re-feel the situation. The resisted feeling becomes apparent, it's always there waiting for you. Don't get sidetracked by trying to understand the history of the feeling. This is often a trick of a mind that loves to think. This over thinking is a form of resistance. If you get tangled up in trying to find a specific name for the feeling, stop. Notice the feeling, idea, or sensation that is present, whether you know what to call it or not. For example, it may be confusion as you find yourself frantically looking for the 'right' feeling. Catching & Releasing the feeling you are in will always bring relief and insight into what is next.

※

You feel for the emotion that goes with the thought that is pronouncing this or that kind of judgment – so you feel that. You bring a vigilance to your inner state. Alertness. You don't demand that you shouldn't be having this thought. It's there. How can you demand you shouldn't be having it if you are having it!? There it is. Suddenly you recognize that this is a thought. And you also recognize the feeling that goes with the thought. How does that feel? You have to see what it feels like. Is it a contraction? Is it turmoil? The moment you direct your attention you realize that you are having this thought. Then the thought no longer has you.

Eckhart Tolle

To apply the Release step, allow the feeling. Relax as much as you can. Take a breath and ease into the sensation of it. Sit in it. Feel it. Look it in the eye for a bit. Breathe it in and willingly experience it with all of the presence you can muster. Be present with it for a minute. There is no wrong way to do this. It can take a few seconds or several minutes. If it is a highly emotional issue and considerably charged it will probably take longer, but not necessarily. You will know. Do it however it works for you. Experiment, and remember feeling something will not destroy or weaken you. This action of allowing will actually make you stronger. Once felt, the sensation can finally move through you instead of being held in place by your resistance to it.

After you have allowed the feeling and you don't feel threatened by it anymore, release when ready. State firmly, "Releasing resentment," or "Releasing this idea of being taken advantage of," use whatever name you gave the sensation. Releasing is a decision, a declaration, and a very powerful one. Decide to Release the idea, feeling, or sensation and then let it go. Letting it go is a choice. If you need something more visual, exhale the feeling, imagine it flowing out of your body and mind, and release it from your cells, your bones, your tissue, and your brain. Students suffering from illness have found this method profoundly helpful.

Note: In the trainings I attended to learn the Yuen Method, with instructor Ishana Bai, we used intention as the single most important aspect of releasing ideas, sensations, or patterns that were destructive. Releasing was a decision to let go, to dismiss, to be done. It was powerful! It was always our declaration that made it so. Dr. Kam Yuen explains throughout his teachings that healing is blocked when a person thinks too much and does not allow himself to feel. His Yuen Method taught how the causes of suffering could be from physical, mental, emotional, psychological or psychic dimensions, in this life or in past lives. The astoundingly simple technique we learned allowed us to release any obstacle to health and happiness regardless of where or when it came from. Success required acknowledging the feeling or idea with a firm intention to let it go. Many students of the Yuen Method added a visual instruction to their body and mind with an authoritative wave of their hand. It was an energetic command to release. There is considerable scientific evidence that demonstrates how hand movement deepens brain integration.

The next step, once you've released the sensation, is to choose the feeling you prefer to have. What would you like to cultivate and flow into your presence, your body, and your awareness? You have a buffet of choices available every moment of life. Being human offers a grand variety! Select the experience you want to let in. Once you decide, imagine the sensation, feel it, and breathe it into your body, your heart, and your mind. Do whatever you need to do to cultivate this feeling and experience it. Allow the new idea to soothe you. If you like, flow it into your cells, bones, and any area of concern.

These are the Catch & Release steps. It's simple and goes like this. Notice you're getting frustrated. Feel your resistance to the feeling. Own the frustration as yours. When complete decide to release it by stating, "releasing resistance to frustration." Notice how you feel.

If a feeling has been haunting you for a long time and collected a large amount of your emotional energy and focus, you may find layers of ideas and sensations connected with it. Don't dismay. Each release and each invitation of a feeling of choice is quite powerful. It's working, don't give up. You might invite someone to sit with you as you apply the steps for support on your first attempt to a highly charged issue. This is a great process to share with friends.

Catch & Release is effective on unhealthy habits, hurtful ideas, doubts, fears, blame, physical pain, non-forgiveness, and any other sensations or ideas you have and no longer want. To the degree you can own the feeling, idea, or sensation is the degree you will be able to release it. If you have difficulty owning something as yours, don't fret we will get to the forgiveness chapter very soon. Chances are if you can't own a sensation or idea and have trouble letting it go, you haven't forgiven yourself or another. Some students have applied the process to the feeling of not wanting to forgive someone and released a significant amount of pain by letting their stubbornness go.

Catch & Release can transform your life in many ways. I love using it on feelings that show up when I begin to resist a fellow human. It moves mountains for me to release the whole business of being critical of someone, it's incredibly kind and freeing. If you have an afternoon and you're in the mood to transform a relationship, apply Catch & Release to any motivation, fear, or sensation you have regarding this person. Do this regarding a stranger, a politician, or co-worker who drives you crazy. Once complete you will have little doubt about the possibilities of this simple process! Blame disappears and a new level of joy and freedom are born.

Within one week of committed practice students noticed a renewed sense of purpose and increased appreciation for self and others. After just one month of applying this process with perseverance magic occurred for many. Relationships that had been difficult or painful showed new possibility as blame was replaced with ownership and compassion. The honesty required for the Catch & Release process to be effective opened unseen and tightly closed doors. Success was inevitable.

When your determination to have compassion and see the good in others supersedes your inclination to criticize or punish them, you have reached one of the pinnacles of being human. There is no turning back. This is one of those bells you can't un-ring once it's been rung. This is evidence that your reality is beginning to shift in a profound way. How? Once we realize feelings come from inside and understand how our thoughts, intentions and words are alive and deeply affect others, we intuitively make corrections.

Become increasingly responsible for how you treat others and how you spend your energy and focus and you will manifest every dream you could ever dream. You cannot separate the two. Responsibility is the ability to respond in the present moment without blame. Manifestation is a result of putting our attention and energy exactly where we choose to.

It is fun and extremely useful learning to pay attention to your modus operandi when faced with discomfort or opposition. These situations will reveal resisted experiences and offer a golden opportunity to recover energy from debilitating habits so you can redirect it toward goals. If you want to become really powerful and clear old patterns or if you find yourself bored and in the mood for developing your skill to decide, direct, and decree… go hang out with someone that annoys you! Watch the news, listen to political campaign commercials, and Catch & Release your reactions so you can no longer feel resentment or resistance toward them. Your particular response or 'avoiding-formula' is good to become aware of. It's exciting to know ourselves!

When faced with an uncomfortable situation, is your automatic reaction to ignore, pretend, blame, criticize, or drink too much? A few feelings that signal me to pay closer attention are; feeling stupid, feeling taken advantage of, wanting to leave abruptly, or pretending to feel a certain way when I don't. If I get the urge to drink copious amounts of red wine or if I'm impatient, it's a signal. These are all indications I am resisting experiencing something. They are worth Catching so I can take responsibility for whatever is consuming my creative energy and move toward solution. Dreams await!

≈

Focus attention on the feeling inside you.

Know that it is the pain-body.

Accept that it is there.

Don't think about it - don't let the feeling turn into thinking.

Don't judge or analyze.

Don't make an identity for yourself out of it.

Stay present, and continue to be the observer of what is happening inside you.

Become aware not only of the emotional pain but also of "the one who observes," the silent watcher.

This is the power of the Now, the power of your own conscious presence.

Then see what happens.

Eckhart Tolle

≈

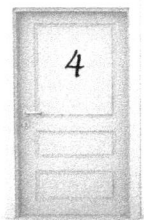

Welcome to Door #4

Catch & Release Exercise

•Select any feeling, idea, or sensation you have caught and would like to release (from previous lists or in the present moment).

•Investigate further by asking, "What feeling, idea, or sensation do I NOT want to have?" Feel your way to the answer, discover what you're resisting.

•Once you become aware of the feeling, idea, or sensation you are avoiding, decide to experience it. Invite it in. Some people find visualizing and breathing the sensation into their body useful. Just let the feeling be there for a minute or two. Allow it to exist. Sit with the experience and it will begin to lessen. Own the feeling, idea, or sensation as completely as you are able to (feelings come from inside). Be present with the sensation until you are complete and no longer experience resistance or fear of this feeling, idea, or sensation. Release it by affirming and state, "Releasing _____." Fill in the blank with the name you've given the feeling. If you don't have a name for it, "Releasing this feeling," is a powerful declaration.

•Select a feeling, idea, or sensation you would like to have. Cultivate it. Recall it from the past if necessary. Decide to saturate your awareness with this sensation. Breathe it in, imagine it soothing you, and allow the feeling to flow into your body, mind, spirit, and heart. Continue soaking in this chosen experience until you are complete.

Example 1

David selected the nagging idea that he isn't doing enough.

David sat quietly in his office and wondered, what feeling do I **not** want to have regarding not doing enough? What am I avoiding? His attention immediately went to a feeling of anxiety, a feeling he often pushed against. He questioned if this was it and asked himself again, "what feeling am I not wanting to have?" Instantly he felt a sensation of losing wealth, losing respect, losing value, and losing hope. It amazed him how quickly the sensation appeared with the asking of the question. He thought it was a strange reply, but it came from him so he decided to stay with this idea. It was disturbing and he began to realize he had resisted this feeling for as long as he could remember. He decided to call the sensation, fear of losing something. He then invited this feeling in. Suddenly his chest felt heavy and he was very uncomfortable. He felt an intense confusion for about ten seconds, almost like a child would. Then anxiety set in. He stayed present, allowing it and owning it as much as he could. He didn't like it at all. He took a deep breath and decided to just let it be there. He relaxed a little more, willing to soak in the anxious feeling. It began to lessen. He wondered where it went. He explored for the feeling of fear around the idea of losing something and found his heart started beating fast. He recalled losing his wallet as a child with all his savings in it. He let the anger and fear be there, he looked it in the eye and sat in it, willingly. It surprised him how easy it became. He was no longer resisting the experience. Not at all. When he felt complete he stated with authority, "Releasing my fear of losing something." He felt the sensation leaving his body. He experienced the power of deciding. He then contemplated losing something and didn't feel afraid of the feeling. The idea he selected to fill up with was feeling successful. He imagined this feeling and it was really easy for him. He sensed the joy of it, how fulfilling it was to allow, and was a bit surprised he could cultivate it. The sensation saturated his presence. He felt happy, and more in control of his life.

Example 2

Sally elected to use Catch & Release with her daughter who was upset about an incident at school.

Sally asked her daughter if she wanted to experiment with this new process she was learning called Catch & Release. She told her it could help her feel better. She explained the steps of the process and how experiencing and feeling what she has been resisting could give her relief. Her daughter agreed but wasn't too enthusiastic about the prospect of feeling pain on purpose, the very pain she had been holding back with all her might. She had been very emotional the last few days over a fight with her best friend. She hadn't wanted to tell her mother all the details so Sally assured her, she didn't need to say anything out loud or explain anything she wasn't ready to reveal during the process.

To begin, Sally invited her daughter to take a deep breath and relax for a minute. She then guided her to recall the moment she began to feel upset. When ready she invited her to just notice the feeling(s) for a minute. She waited until she felt her daughter was experiencing the event and then asked her, "What feeling are you NOT wanting to have in all this? Investigate for a minute. What are you trying to avoid experiencing?" She told her daughter she didn't need to say it out loud. She openly reported to her mom she didn't want to feel all the sad feelings. Her mom then invited her to just let that sad feeling be there, she told her to let it exist for a minute so she could stop being afraid of it. "Look it in the eye, breathe it in and let it be alive in you instead of trying not to feel it." Her daughter squirmed a little but willingly began to allow it. She started to weep and feel the despair. Then she opened her eyes and said, "now what?" Her mom asked her if she still felt it and she replied, "not very much," so her mom invited her to look at it again and see what was there and include it, "feel it the best you can. And then decide to release anything that's left by imagining it flowing out of

When a person is dealing with an emotional event it is supportive and kind to have a guide. Please note, this process is not to replace professional counsel of any kind. If you are in the care of a therapist review the process with them before you begin.

you, out of your legs; imagine this feeling leaving your mind and body. When you are ready, state with authority, Releasing sadness." The daughter was quiet for a minute longer and then stated firmly, "Releasing sadness." Sally was very present watching. Her daughter looked up and asked, "what just happened?" Sally explained, "feelings come from inside, not from what is happening outside. It's our opinions of what is happening that hurt so bad. I am learning we get to be in charge of how we see things and how we hold onto feelings." The daughter seemed to like this idea. Sally then suggested her daughter begin to create feeling how she wanted to feel now and then, just for fun. She asked her if she could choose a feeling to have right now, what would she pick? Her daughter responded quickly, "Not worrying." Her mom then asked, "What would that feel like, to not worry?" She answered, "calm and peaceful." Sally invited her daughter to close her eyes and imagine what being calm and peaceful felt like, to imagine her body and mind filling with this sensation of peace, to let it flow into her and soothe her. She told her daughter to create the feelings the best she could and let them fill her senses. Sally could feel the peace and calm filling the space. Her daughter's expression changed and Sally appreciated her being so open and willing. It was a very special moment. As her daughter opened her eyes Sally encouraged her further, "You can do this anytime you feel stuck in a feeling honey. You get to pick what you focus on. Let me know if you ever need any help." The daughter felt very different, more in charge, less of a victim. She hugged her mom with all her heart.

Catch & Release Success Stories

Dear Holly... I was skiing last weekend and while on the chair my husband told me some upsetting news about my son. In a nutshell, it was a description of how much of a loner my son still is in life. He described how my son doesn't really fit in. It hit a very old soft spot for me. Rather than try to explain it away or immediately look on the bright side of it (like I normally would) I stopped, and *told my husband that I needed a minute to practice what I'd been learning. I asked myself what I was trying not to feel and it was right there, failure as a mother. I used the Catch & Release to release FAILURE. I opened up my chest, let it in big time, and I consciously told my supremely wise, higher self awareness to deal with it and just allow it to exist. I kept breathing it in. Guess what, I felt it and it couldn't hurt me, not anymore! Wonder of wonders....all this time I'd been running away from it, by pushing it aside in favor of some positive thoughts, but this time I just let those %$#@*& thoughts IN. My higher self, with its divine wisdom, had everything it needed to fully experience the pain.*

Once I felt a huge decrease in the charge, once it felt like it had passed, I simply had a second conversation with my cells, my DNA, and consciously brought in TRUST. Trust in myself, trust in my son, trust in the universe, trust in where this was all leading. This sounds long, but it was quick. I finished before we got off the lift. I felt better. Not ecstatic, not blissful, but most assuredly better. We kept skiing, and a while later I got this huge hit of insight about energy management. It seems so obvious now when I write this, but I was feeling how by pushing yucky stuff away, we have to expend energy to keep it at a distance. To keep it pushed away uses my power. Over and over....every time I think about the offending subject, the feeling I didn't want to have would peek in, and I'd quickly move it aside and cover it up with a better feeling thought, all the while still spending energy to push it away. My own positive thinking was exhausting me. By letting it in, allowing it, feeling it, and letting it have its way briefly, I ended up just sitting calmly inside myself still holding all of my precious energy!

You've probably said this multiple times to me, but I have to tell you that it really clicked for me! It's so obvious, simple and beautiful. And while it's resonant with Abraham-Hicks work, it provides that crucial piece of allowing it BEFORE you find the better feeling thought, which preserves the life energy. WOW! Thank you so much. My life is transforming – E.H.

～～

Dear Holly... I want to tell you about a wonderful experience that I had with "Catch & Release" in the context of education. One of my special needs students has recently experienced a divorce in her family. This week she came into class and continued to say, "I can't do it. I'm sad." I used my usual strategies of redirecting and assisting, but she insisted on feeling sad (very intuitive on her part). I asked her to meet with me during recess so we could talk about her sadness. She smiled for the first time all week. At recess we sat down and I invited her, "Okay, let's feel sad together. What does sadness feel like? Close your eyes and let's really feel it together." She did it. Earlier during the recess I had retrieved a stick that a boy was flinging around. So I improvised and used the stick as a wand saying, "Let's magically wave these feelings away and let them go."

"Poof. They're gone." My student looked up to me and started giggling.

"What are some good feelings that we can fill ourselves with?" I questioned.

The little girl said, "I don't know."

"Who do you feel loved by?" I invited.

She answered, "My mommy and my daddy."

"Let's feel that feeling of being loved," I replied. I waved the "wand" around again just for fun...

Her whole body language changed and at the end of recess she skipped back to class. It was wonderfully healing for me as much as her.

I had a great experience with my student AND... I still felt myself resisting my own feelings this week. I didn't want to Catch & Release, so I resorted to my old MO- being busy and feeling numb. I do know that I have increased awareness now. I am aware that I was resisting. Before, I would blame these feelings on various situations. I am working on step one, recognizing and finally acknowledging the fact that I can catch myself resisting. Giving myself credit for this is proving very valuable. I am very hopeful – K.T.

For a more thorough examination and elimination of beliefs, feelings, ideas, and sensations and to discover their origin, programs such as The Avatar Training, www.TheAvatarCourse.com and Byron Katie's, "The Work" www.TheWork.com are exemplary. To explore the Yuen Method go to www.YuenMethod.com or Ishana Bai at www.Te-Energetics.com

• *There may be times that you don't want to let go of pain and you feel a need to wallow in it for a while. Allowing your own suffering to exist can be a very kind act. Understanding that this is one of the choices you have is important. When you sincerely recognize that continuing to hurt is more your decision than the result of someone outside of you forcing an experience on you... be ready for a visceral experience of your power.*

Honor

• *Honor yourself. Giving yourself permission to hurt is not a small thing. Deciding when you are done is monumentally prolific.*

• *There is one requirement so forward motion and relief can occur, it is your willingness to feel. Some like to experience a sensation all at once and some like to allow a small portion at a time. You decide what works best for you. You will know when you are complete, your attention will be more relaxed and neutral. You'll no longer feel upset by the feeling.*

• *Breathing in an experience of choice after each release (and anytime in between) will ignite a new vibration. Begin to experience this inside and it will begin to show up outside. Don't skip this step, it replaces uncertainty with possibility.*

CHAPTER FIVE

Resistance... Catching the Thief

This bandit is sneaky, slippery, quick, and debilitating. The most challenging characteristic of this smooth criminal, the one that makes him hard to identify, is how absolutely accepted he is. The moment we call him by name he mysteriously births justification. A skilled master of illusion and transparency, well versed in generating and collecting agreement. He wears many faces. You may have known him as anger, unfairness, disease, corruption, addiction, pain, or loss... just to name a few. His real name is Resistance.

Resisting reality is the number one culprit of misery. Reality being anything and everything, whether imagined or real, that we are facing. Resisting hurts worse, lasts longer, and disables success significantly more than allowing an experience to exist ever could.

There is a very interesting phenomenon regarding resistance that is often overlooked. When we resist something we actually glue ourselves to it. When we push against a reality we give that exact reality a portion of ourselves. Here's how... in order to hold something at bay (a feeling, a person, an idea, a pain, an event, the past, etc.) we must constantly flow a little stream of attention in its direction. To manage it and try and keep it at a distance, we must give it a flow of our energy. Even an effort to ignore a person, place, or thing requires continual management of it.

– The third of Sir Issac Newton's law of physics states, *"For every action there is an equal and opposite reaction..."* *For every force there is an equal and opposite force. For example, if you push on a wall, it will push back on you as hard as you are pushing on it. And you and the wall will stay in place.*

– Abraham Hicks explains it like this, *"As you position yourself against SOME thing that SOME thing gets stronger—and you hold yourself separate from solution."*

– Werner Erhard often said, *"The best way to make something persist is to resist it."*

Many great teachers say it many ways but it boils down to this, resistance is the most overlooked obstacle to success, healing, and creating fulfilling relationships.

It's better to experience this phenomenon than read about it. Explore by holding up your left hand. Consider this hand something you resist in life, maybe a pain, a notion of failure, an event from the past, being sick, losing money, being lonely, a person, etc. Use something real for you. Now, hold up your right hand and think of this hand as you. Take your right hand (you) and press it against the left hand (the reality you are resisting). Go ahead and literally push against and hold back the reality you don't like. Keep pressing against this 'thing' just enough to keep it at bay. Use one finger for a full minute and maintain a steady amount of force to keep that darn thing right where you want it, away from you! Resisting this reality uses your creative energy. Multiply the consumption of energy by the number of realities you are resisting in life.

What are YOU touching in order to hold it back? What is required of YOUR attention to continue resisting, ignoring, managing, not liking, criticizing, keeping an eye on, this feeling, person, or situation you abhor? What do YOU have to do with your energy in order to make sure you avoid the reality? What are you gluing yourself to with your resistance? What are you giving your valueable creative energy to?

≈≈

Whoever or whatever attention is placed on becomes more real.

Harry Palmer
Resurfacing, Techniques for Exploring Consciousness

≈≈

If someone really understands and implements this quote from Harry Palmer, they don't need to read another line in this book. The mistaken notion is that by resisting something we are keeping it away from us. Oddly we conclude that if we resist something, it will never get us! As Sir Issac Newton's law of physics explains, nothing could be further from the truth. The resisted reality is already devouring/getting us via our unconscious involvement with it! Our resistance actually keeps the very thing we are resisting in our energy field, in our presence! Our pushing against something feeds it, keeps it alive and snuggled up against us! Resistance is not a passive act. We do it so automatically that we don't realize the drain it is on our power and ability to manifest desires ... until we stop!

There are many faces of resistance and they can be quick and slippery when we reach to admit and own them in ourselves. It takes willingness and honesty to acknowledge when we're caught up in a game of pushing against something. Attributes of resistance include avoiding, blaming, ignoring, resenting, bull headedness, over eating, over sexing, over televisioning, over consuming, criticizing, pretending, insisting on being right, not wanting to feel wrong, punishing, and any other type of self-righteous behavior. When engaged in one of these resistant activities there is usually a fear or worry about feeling a specific sensation or experiencing a certain reality. Resisting is an act of trying NOT to allow an experience, idea, or feeling to exist... when it already does exist.

⌒⌒

When I argue with reality, I lose—but only 100% of the time.

Byron Katie

⌒⌒

Note - resistance is different from a deliberate intention to examine a problem and produce solutions. Resistance is exhausting. Resistance does not create relief. Typically when we are pushing against something we become over stimulated, emotional, and positional. Resistance is a repetitive and automatic act, often unconscious, yet almost always justified. Resistance continues through time. In contrast, a deliberate investigation into issues with an intention to rectify has a noticeable beginning and end in time. A purposeful investigation is rewarding, fulfilling, and reveals intuitive direction.

To repeatedly criticize or dislike something depletes energy. Considering it, analyzing it, and doing what needs to be done to continually prove its flaw or unworthiness is grueling. This is how resistance works. It can include reading books on the rightness of our viewpoints (there are books to prove most any perspective), joining groups and finding friends that support our resistant actions (there are groups/people who will support most any perspective), and using our time to collect agreement on how wrong something is. A mind/ego loves being right about what's wrong, having consensus, and feeling like an authority on something. We are not our minds or our thoughts.

Spreading 'wrongness' every chance we get is not fulfilling work.

Sometimes a thought is relatively harmless and you can justifiably say, "I am having a thought." But at others times, when you are not having a thought, but the thought has you ... how do you know this is happening? You don't even know you are having a thought! You are so identified with the thought that whatever judgment this thought pronounces upon the world, you believe to be absolute reality!

Eckhart Tolle

It is such an automatic response to resist a reality that doesn't fit into our picture of what is fair, right, and good. Understandably, we are quick to resist certain perspectives. Pain, death, and suffering are not concepts we have learned how to integrate or comprehend, so we naturally try to steer clear of them. They hurt, but they do exist! What we were never educated to understand is the cost of our resistance and how it prolongs our suffering. We aren't aware of the doors we close with our opposition and avoidance to our feelings or how it blocks discovery of peaceful solution. Resistance obstructs the intuitive insight that becomes available when we are open and allowing. We are unaware of the investment we make into sustaining the very thing we resist by hating it, pushing against it, and continually telling our sad or blame filled stories. Please note, repeatedly telling the same story is not to be confused with expressing ourselves because we need to talk and have someone listen. Expressing ourselves and telling another how we feel deep inside is a very powerful form of releasing pain as well.

Even though we were taught to be tougher than hardship and instructed to become adept at resisting as a strategy to succeed in life, we often suffer secretly so nobody can witness our pain. We were never taught how to manage discouragement, disappointment, or heartache in an efficient manner. We haven't been comfortable admitting these feelings exist, too afraid of what will be thought of us. Uninformed, we didn't realize that pushing against reluctance, hating anger, or pretending sadness isn't there, actually made things worse. The tucked away resistance grew into an obstacle that became harder to manage down the road.

> *Some people resist change*
> *Some resist pain*
> *Some resist hard work*
> *Some resist certain food*
> *Some resist political figures*
> *Some resist certain types of people*
> *Some resist men/women*
> *Some resist failure*
> *Some resist intimacy*
> *Some people resist themselves*

It is never the subject of our resistance that steals our life energy. It is our decision to focus on what we consider 'wrong or unjust' that is the true thief. It is the decision to resist that destroys the spirit… it is never the issue at hand.

Repeatedly pushing against something attracts more of what we resist and sabotages possibility and solution. Resisting is hard on our health and leaves us exhausted, unfulfilled, and frustrated. Which begs the question, are you wasting any of your creative energy resisting? Are there certain aspects of your life you find yourself repeatedly pushing against?

Letting go of resistance has miraculous results when it comes to manifesting abundance, passion, and attracting fulfilling relationships both professionally and personally. Releasing resistance allows nourishment into every facet of creating a satisfying life. Imagine a person who has resisted the idea of failing or not being good enough since they were a wee little one. Feel how this fear could infiltrate every aspect and decision of their life; career choice, self-expression, choosing a partner, investments, and all the doors they never knocked on. They would make the fearful choice rather than the passionate or authentic one. Authentic living always results in possibility. Fearful living always results in fearful living.

Now imagine who this person would be without the fear. How would they feel? What would they want? How big would their dreams be? I believe if they applied Catch & Release to their resistance to failure and let go of the associated feelings, something spectacular would happen.

They would be free. They would be present in the moment making brilliant choices from current data (people free of resistance see possibility everywhere they look). Like magic they would know the next action needed that would be best for all concerned. Motivated by wisdom and passion, their health and vitality are awakened, fun is the name of the game, and going for dreams is all there is to do!

Resistance dissolves, melts, and disappears with each and every moment of allowing.

Looking into the eye of what we're resisting is how we can know it is an idea or feeling we are afraid of and not an incident in present time. As we comprehend the simplicity of this notion, resistance rarely steals our peace of mind. If it does it is very brief, we simply apply Catch & Release and cultivate presence, trust, or cooperation in its place. This is power.

Imagine alowing the sensation of failure to exist for a minute so you can recover the energy you're spending on resisting this feeling. You'll move forward no longer operating out of fear. With practice you'll become clear in your ability to Catch & Release doubts, fears, and worry. You will easily access a strong and authentic belief in your ability to focus, to apply what you know and trust your decision. You become certain no matter what shows up in the future you will be ready for it. You'll be present and unafraid of a feeling that MAY occur.

Now you get to decide, heartily, not to waste another moment of your life resisting what could or might happen because you understand… every drop of worry about the future is robbing you of the wisdom and power of today. You no longer operate your business, your relationships, or your body with resistance to failure as your motivation. Consider the possibilities when all that energy recovered from resisting is refocused toward designing success, finding solutions, and seizing opportunities. You feel more alive, freer, and willing to explore like you did when you were a child. Your state of mind and enthusiasm attract new clients, better health, and sweet dreams when your head hits the pillow.

"When we stop opposing reality, action becomes simple, fluid, kind, and fearless."

Byron Katie

Examples of Resistance

Physically… A young gal often has a stomach ache. She hates it, ignores it, and does her best to pretend it isn't there. It annoys her but she doesn't allow the feelings to exist. She criticizes herself, her body, flowing anger toward her life and her belly. She resists her body.

Mentally… Reoccurring blame, judgment of another, self or the world… "It is my father's fault I am so cold hearted." "The economy will never recover." "I am not good at this." "I hate making cold calls." "Life is hard." "It's the government's fault." "It's my ex-partner's fault."

Emotionally… A partner comes home two hours later than promised. The one waiting stews, blames, over eats, drinks, thinks vengeful thoughts or maybe pretends it doesn't matter, goes numb and deliberately betrays the partner as punishment.

Resistance is any action done to cover up, deny, avoid, or pretend a feeling isn't there.

Example of Resistance in Business

While working with a client who was very determined to manifest more wealth, something quite interesting was revealed. As we explored obstacles he discovered that his anger and frustration (resistance) were consuming a large portion of his ability to create the forward motion he knew he was capable of. As he became honest about how he was spending his time he realized he had more attention and energy keeping an eye on his competitors than he was actually directing toward his own goals. He was constantly checking on the success of 'others' and kept a mind full of notes on the unethical practices he witnessed to prove there was no justice in their many accomplishments! He collected this data and waved it around whenever an opportunity to defend his failure appeared… all the while steaming over the money rolling into his competition's bank account. When he realized he was resisting his competitor, more than designing his own success, he understood it was his focus on what wasn't working that had stolen his power to succeed. His resistance had consumed all his creative energy and almost destroyed his company's future. Once he understood how his resistance actually fed the very feeling he wanted to get away from (the ideas, sensations, and feelings of unfairness and not being good enough were the areas we addressed), he became committed to the Catch & Release process you're learning in this handbook. He transformed his habitual criticism and comparing himself to others into orchestrating success. He became energized and optimistic by focusing on creating and implementing a plan of action instead of wasting his power on resisting and constantly noticing what was wrong. He avidly practiced Catching his 'make wrong' habit and released it so he could put his power into an item on his action list. Promoting, inspiring, and empowering his employees was a large part of his plan. Once he realized they were modeling his focus of attention, noticing what was 'wrong' with their peers and the industry, he took responsibility for helping them recognize and imagine possibilities in its place. He realized if he wanted to enjoy success one of the best avenues was by helping others to succeed. His perseverance with Catch & Release transformed many of his relationships, especially with his wife and children. He had no idea the amount of energy he had been channeling into what wasn't working, what he didn't like, and how wrong everyone was.

Example of Resistance in the body

When in the hospital the pain in my abdomen was excruciating. I resisted it with all my might. I hated how it took over my body and I had no control. I wanted it gone and didn't want anyone to know that I couldn't handle my pain. I was embarrassed that I was hurting, as though it was wrong and a sign of weakness. I wanted to keep my suffering a secret to avoid the ridicule I was certain would come from others. I tried everything I knew to run away from my pain. I ignored it, hated it, blamed it and refused it. I continually felt like a victim and that having a disease was horribly unfair. I blamed my upbringing and God for where I found myself. Until a dear friend, my sister, sat with me and said these magic words, "Your resistance is making it worse. You have to look the pain in the eye, breathe it in and let it be there. Stop pushing against it. Invite it in."

I thought she was crazy. But I didn't have anything to lose so I tried it. She sat with me and guided me. Softly she said, "Let it be there, stop hating it. Breathe it in like you ordered it for dinner." I felt lost, had no idea how to do this but I tried. I closed my eyes and put all my focus where the pain was in my stomach. I felt it, probably for the first time without hating it. She nudged me further. "Feel it now, allow it and listen to it. Become the pain, feel where it is located and what it is touching. Now **be it** completely, just **become it** and breathe it all in. Keep doing this until you are no longer afraid of its existence."

She coached me through this process several times and miraculously my discomfort subsided a little more with each breath I took. Merging with the pain transformed my resistance to it. I am positive it was my resistance making it hurt so unbearably. By inviting the pain to be there, staying present with it, the discomfort loosened its hold and it became tolerable. I no longer felt out of control. It was as though my resistance held my misery in place and allowing it to exist helped it relax. I was astounded. Pain became something I didn't need to fear or push against ever again. It was just pain. It needed to be felt to be set free.

I learned to breathe it in and breathe it out. I let it move through me. I ended up with a lot of free energy to direct toward healing instead of being oriented to what I didn't want. Allowing was the opposite of resisting. It wasn't a push, a force, or an action. It was opening up to what was occurring, with no judgment of it being good or bad. Allowing was much easier than resisting. Allowing is an art worth learning.

This process of healing is outlined thoroughly in my book, *Allowing A Portrait of Forgiving and Letting Life Love You.*

Welcome to Door #5

Transform Resistance Into Dreams

•Scan your work/home environment, relationships, and your body. List ideas, feelings, and sensations you resist.

•Apply Catch & Release to your list of resisted realities. No hurry, this is a process you will use for the rest of your life. Let it be easy. Sometimes simply listing the items is enough. You decide. Handle one item at a time by asking, "What feeling, idea, or sensation am I resisting and not wanting to have regarding the item? Once identified, feel the discovered idea, feeling, or sensation you have been resisting. Allow it for a minute, breathe it in and let it exist. When ready, decide to release it by stating, "Releasing _____." Fill in the blank with the name of the feeling, idea, or sensation. Select a feeling of choice to refill with. Begin imagining it, cultivate it and feel it. Let it saturate your senses.

Enjoy the fact that you just created a new feeling. This will become easy and natural after a few applications. Your tendency to Catch & Release will replace any propensity to resist once you experience the relief and happiness that accompanies allowing.

To review a thorough explanation of the Catch & Release steps refer to chapter 4-Catch & Release, page 42.

Example 1

David listed – I resist John, inefficiency, wasting time, not exercising daily, sitting in front of the television, not having sex, eating too much, people not doing what is expected of them, dishonesty, pretense, and being taken advantage of.

David took the most disturbing item on his list to see if this process would work. He was doubtful he would be able to let go of this lifelong plague of despising dishonesty. He took a deep breath and tried to relax for a minute so his mind would become more still. He then brought up his idea of dishonesty and it immediately went to an individual who had lied to him about joining his team. He believed this person manipulated him to gain information knowing he would later make up an excuse for not being able to follow through. David felt duped, tricked and got lost in this for a moment before he asked himself the question, "What feeling am I not wanting to have?" The answer came quickly, it was feeling stupid. This is an experience he had resisted since grade school. He decided to go for it and finally feel it. He had to settle down for a minute because the resistance was pretty strong and included some anger. He took another deep breath to relax and repeated the words to himself, feeling stupid, being stupid, stupid…. He slowly allowed himself to drop into the sensation. It was very uncomfortable yet he told himself, "let it be there for a minute, it's not going to kill you." He felt it. It was very interesting to him to just let it be without pushing it aside. He had denied this feeling existed inside of him for a very long time. He felt stupid and he started to laugh at how stupid it was to sit down and deliberately feel stupid.

He gathered himself and looked to see if he was pushing against this sensation anymore, and he wasn't. He understood how having a feeling of being stupid for a couple of minutes was much easier than running from it for so long. He realized resisting feeling stupid would never control him again. He felt very present and compassionate. Not just for himself, he thought of all the people being chased through life by a feeling. He imagined everyone running from feeling stupid and just shook his head. He felt free and excited about letting go of the resistance on his list. Then he remembered to pick a feeling he wanted to have. He chose having faith in himself. He smiled before beginning, liking his choice. He imagined what it would feel like to let this feeling in and really own it. He felt the sensations of believing in himself with a flavor of trusting himself almost instantly. He invited these ideas to saturate his senses. He really enjoyed cultivating this feeling of having faith in his SELF. He felt calm, present, and able. He realized this feeling could transform how he related to his team, his partner, and his family. He decided to cultivate this feeling more often.

Example 2

Sally listed – More than anything I resist being ignored and not listened to, this happens all the time with my family and my friends. I resist conflict, insincerity, and people who say they will do something and then they don't. My daughter suffering is unbearable for me. I resist what people are doing to the earth; I resist waste, over consumption, and ignorance. I hate the excessive benefit packages of our government officials when this is unavailable to the people of our country. I resist being manipulated by advertising and how this affects impressionable minds. I resist cruelty to animals and suffer over this greatly. I AM CONSUMED BY MY RESISTANCE!!!

Sally selected her resistance to being ignored for her first item. She took a few deep breaths to relax determined to become the observer of her thoughts rather than get caught up in them. She knew being present made it easier to feel a sensation. She meditated for a couple of minutes and when her mind became quiet she brought up the idea of being ignored and immediately felt a pang of sadness in her chest. Her mind wanted to blame her parents and her siblings but she caught the conversation starting and whispered out loud, "feel how you resist being ignored." She felt her resistance, it was intense. It was a mix of anger, blame, and sadness. She had trouble separating the feelings. She couldn't give the sensation one name. She kept feeling how much she hated being left out, not included, and ignored. She took a very long slow deep breath and let the anger be there. She looked her resistance (anger) right in the eye and stayed very present with it, and experienced it until it lessened. She started to cry as a wave of tremendous sadness moved through her. She surrendered and let it all be there... she felt, she waited, and she allowed. Everything became calm and still. Eager to discover any remains she deepened her awareness and invited all her resistance to being ignored to reveal itself. Many sensations moved through her and she just let them be there. It took a while.

NOTE - Sally ended up addressing many feelings at once. This can be effective for some and not for others. You have to explore what works best for you. One feeling at a time is most efficient and thorough in my experience.

Sally continued, wanting to release everything she was

feeling. She felt like she had reached a satisfactory place. She was ready and had become quiet in her mind. She felt her own presence for a moment and decided with conviction, "Releasing my resistance to being ignored." She imagined all the feelings flowing out of her body, out of her mind, and through her legs into the earth below. When done, she scanned to see if anything remained. She felt relief but doubted that the whole pile of resistance was gone. She wasn't sure it could be that easy. She felt her body and mind again looking for resistance to being ignored. She was certain about one thing, she wasn't afraid of feeling ignored... not anymore. If it showed up in the future, she was ready! She almost wished someone was home so she could ask them to ignore her just to see how she felt in that moment. She laughed at her thought! She decided she was complete for now with the release and concluded if the resistance showed up again she would feel it and release it. She had an insight about doubting, self-doubt was very familiar to her. She promised herself she would take 'doubt' through Catch & Release.

She felt good about her effort and picked liking herself as her feeling of choice. She smiled even before beginning. She imagined being kind to herself, seeing the good in herself, and treating herself with honor, and... no longer ignoring herself. She began flowing a river of kind attention toward her body, her life, and took a few moments to acknowledge her determination to be a good person. She giggled. She felt how life could be very sweet, if she let it.

Kindness

When a person is hurting, repeating an old story, and unable to stop the suffering associated with the telling of it … it is a kind act to pose the question, "What are you trying not to feel?" Or ask, "What sensation do you want to avoid?" Give them a moment, they may need to explore for a bit. Then invite them to take a deep breath and just allow the sensation to exist for a few seconds so they can stop running from it. Help them look the feeling in the eye and simply be with it. It is the running which hurts so badly. Feelings will pass with ownership. Running away can last forever.

Holly Riley

CHAPTER SIX

Thoughts, Feelings, and Intentions are ALIVE!

My collapsed body was on the floor below, shrinking from view as I moved further and further away. There was a deep knowing in me that I needed to travel in a specific direction... I was being summoned. I intuitively turned toward an opening up ahead. There was a brilliant and soothing light streaming through. I was floating, being drawn toward the sensation. It was as though it was singing to me. It was far, then close, and in a flash appeared even further in the distance. I struggled to get closer. It was so difficult to propel myself forward; everything was happening in slow, slow motion. Still, I had no doubt I was in the right place.

I could see a group of people up ahead, everyone adorned in white or perhaps it was the brilliant light shining around each person that made them look transparent. I strained to see more clearly and they all seemed illuminated from both the inside and the outside. Curious, I continued moving toward the amazing sensations that seemed to be coming from them. They were electric, vibrating, and so happy. I got close enough to see that they were all excitedly staring toward the center of a large circle that was about ten people deep. It felt as though they were combining their focus like a river toward some 'thing' they were all enjoying and appreciating. The sensation flowing from them was pure and full of joy! I couldn't figure out what all the hubbub was about so I very determinedly tried to get even closer. I wanted to find out what was receiving that buzz of energy. I longed to move nearer to them but my body would not obey. Everyone was laughing and embracing one another with so much love, they seemed like one large entity split up into smaller parts, but still connected! It was as if the whole group was holding one paintbrush, designing an enchanting new piece of art as a team, and operating with one mind. I wanted to be part of that circle!

Suddenly a man on the outer edge of the crowd turned and saw me, he seemed surprised and quickly advanced in my direction. I didn't recognize his face but I was certain I'd known him before. Somehow I recalled the feeling of him, his spirit, his energy, and his demeanor. I just couldn't place where from. I appreciated his presence moving nearer, it was familiar and comfortable like home. As he departed from the group the entire circle turned to see what had transpired. Instantly the crowd moved toward me and clapped their hands as if celebrating. They all cheered and laughed like they were thrilled to see me. They all came close to hug me. Each of them flowing compassion like a river into my awareness. They were old friends. I knew them all, but their faces were different. The sensations that caressed me with each embrace are still part of my heart. Each *Being* shared a feeling of appreciation that imprinted my soul as they hugged me. It was familial and forever. The current vibrated through my core. Being close to them was wordless and true. I had forgotten this feeling existed deep inside of me. I had forgotten this feeling was/is the greater truth of existence.

The *Being* that first saw me gently but authoritatively took me by the shoulders and turned me back toward the direction I came from. He steered me away from the group. He stayed close, right beside me, and we traveled much faster than I had alone. Suddenly, there was an opening in a cloud in front of us. It was a window of sorts and I wasn't sure where we were going. He seemed in a hurry. Then I saw my body lying on the floor below us and I understood where I was, or better said, where I wasn't. There were medics leaning over my body and my leg was twisted up backward, it looked weird and contorted. It was surreal like I was watching a silent movie. I had no emotion about any of it until we moved close enough for me to see my son's face. Drake was standing off to the side with my mother. That is when my understanding of life changed forever.

I looked at Drake and what I saw was his brilliant and shiny spirit. It was vast, huge and connected into what I will call Divine Intelligence. He was so perfect, his beingness intensely alive and aware. He was totally connected to the grid, to the flow of life, to All That Is. He was complete. I felt his magnificence so deeply that my faith in him and all humans, became even more solid. I looked at my dear mother and like Drake, she was intrinsically linked to what mattered most. The field that goes on forever and connects us all. She was amazing, wonderful, and whole, and always would be. This I knew. The real profundity was that the bodies below thought the drama and excitement they were shuffling around in a rock hard real reality, when the indisputable truth was that each actor's movie would have a happy ending. It was like a drama and everyone was playing their part famously, only they'd forgotten one very important piece of information: They'd cast themselves into the roles they were playing. They had become the actors so sufficiently and completely that they forgot the larger part of themselves! It was undeniably apparent! I turned to the man standing next to me in utter shock and blurted, "They think it's real!" He looked at me with remarkable compassion and nodded his head slowly as if to solemnly agree.

We moved even closer and as I scanned the other beings below I realized one of them was frail, disconnected, with only a tiny wisp of energy moving between his body and the vastness everyone else was tapped into. At once my awareness was consumed by his field, his body, and his pain. I understood its origin and felt it as my own. Everyone else disappeared to me and I longed to tell this young man who he really was and that he could let go of what was hurting him if he would only remember how powerful he is. Urgency bubbled up from inside of me. I had to let him know that this stream of potential and happiness I was floating in was his, ours, everyone's, just for the asking. I looked over at my guide and he was staring, feeling, and knowing my every thought. As if to fill me up for the next leg of my journey, he poured an inexpressible sensation of grace into me with his loving eyes, he embraced me with his presence and filled me with remembering.

Instantly, I was back in my body. The medic I longed to

encourage was leaning over me. I gazed into his soft blue eyes and smiled with a full heart and a mission… to remind him.

I was back in the same body, but I was not the same 'me.' I was a more expanded version if that makes sense. I understood how every thought, intention and idea we have is not only alive, it moves out from us like ripples in a still pond when a rock is tossed in. I realized we could each add something very important to the world with our happiness and create miracles. But, only to the degree that we believed we could. I understood that becoming aware enough to tap into this powerful energy was available to every living person. I was certain, anybody willing to own where they found themselves and what they were feeling could manifest their dreams.

I realized the EMT leaning over me needed a kind nudge, a reminder of how powerful the focus of his energy and attention were. I planned to let him know that if he kept putting his life force into all those sad and self condemning thoughts, he would never be free. He just needed someone to prod him toward seeing that he was not the painful ideas and opinions he was having but rather the thinker and container of them… and that he could choose something different! I was thrilled to oblige!

I smiled.

∽∼

You can only see what you believe—nothing else is possible

Byron Katie

∽∼

The word attention is derived from two Latin words, ad meaning toward and tendere *meaning to stretch. When you put your attention on something, you stretch toward it.*

Harry Palmer

∽∼

The state of your life is nothing more than a reflection of the state of your mind.

Wayne W. Dyer

∽∼

⌒⌒

Genius is being able to put your attention on a subject, idea, or reality of choice.

Abraham-Hicks

⌒⌒

There's a 'self' in every thought that arises. And there is an absolute conviction in this identification that 'this' thought is absolutely the reality. So here, as an initial exercise, I suggest that you have a little look inside and see whether, perhaps, a thought is having you.

Eckhart Tolle

⌒⌒

Mind undoubtedly is the mechanism of the past and it keeps us firmly bound to the past. Mind is the arch creator of bondages. Whatever we think about becomes our bondage.

Sudharta S.D.

⌒⌒

CHAPTER SEVEN

We are NOT our thoughts

The ideas, notions, and conclusions we have each personally collected are neatly filed, categorized, and retrievable as needed. We're so efficient with our inventory that we can access, spout, and prove the value of our supply at the drop of a hat.

We have thoughts, we become thoughts, we resist thoughts, and we desire thoughts. We try to invest in 'good' thoughts and ignore 'bad' thoughts, and for the most part end up somewhere between the two. We discard the old, no longer useful ones (if we're conscious), and begin collecting data to prove the newly acquired ones we believe are worthy of our focus. Psychological studies show that many continue thinking in the same manner they always have even in the face of evidence proving their thoughts are falsehoods! A habit worth catching.

Thoughts are interesting things. We have them, they come and go, yet some of the very old 'spoon fed' ones have been part of us for so long, we think they are who we are. We can't or don't ever imagine who we would be without them. For example, there are some religious beliefs that many people were taught to honor as absolute truth. They were raised with these ideals. As children we are often fed our parents beliefs just like we are fed dinner. This isn't a bad thing, it is just worth noticing.

Thoughts are alive, they become feelings and manifest into solid realities. Then we protect them and defend them as though our salvation depends upon their survival. We learn to adopt what is handed down to us out of respect for those we love and also as means for gaining approval. We have to wonder about one significant detail… people on the other side of the world, street, and supermarket are being taught very different truths and are instructed by their culture, parents and teachers, that they *must* embrace these very important ideas if they want salvation, good grades, or approval.

Who has the correct thoughts? Which ones are worth fighting for? Are there any worth killing over? Who decides? Had you been born on the other side of the world, would you now be fighting for what that culture holds dear?

If a person has been conditioned from an early age to believe the world is a friendly place, they may have thoughts of kinship and appreciation that naturally occur. When a person is taught from an early age never to trust people, they are conditioned to have fearful thoughts, ideas of losing things and being betrayed. They keep a steadfast eye on windows and doors to make sure they're locked.

The thoughts we habitually think have very much to do with our experience of life. When I was young my dad taught me to pay attention to emotions and streams of thought. "Watch um, watch um," He would chuckle and interrupt right in the middle of some story I was determined to dramatize. He reminded me often, "stay present without being seduced by your own story." He called the emotions I would get stuck in, "Not I's." He would invite me, right in the middle of my brood, to become the watcher of the "Not I's," explaining how this would help me become free of my story. He believed I would find the truth I was hungry to know about life with this practice of identifying "Not I's." All I had to do was discover the watcher of them. It was work.

Dad derived his early understanding of "Not I's" from the teachings of G.I. Gurdjieff, the great master of Self Remembering, whose many works included practices to discover personalities, identities, and habits as separate from our true SELF. Gurdjieff's school of thought taught methods, attention exercises and mind management strategies to help students become aware of who they were beyond ideas, personalities, or conclusions.

⌒⌒

The Many 'I's

Many I's is a term which indicates the different feelings and thoughts of 'I' in a person: I think, I want, I know best, I prefer, I am happy, I am hungry, I am tired, etc. These feelings and thoughts of 'I' usually have nothing in common with one another, and are present for short periods of time. Man has no unity in himself. This lack of unity results in wanting one thing now, and another, perhaps contradictory, thing later.

G.I. Gurdjieff

Food for thought... thoughts can be examined and experienced by us which means we must somehow be separate from them. We can exchange old thoughts for new thoughts, agree with certain ones while refusing others. Thus, we have the capacity to choose! If two people feel the exact same thought in opposition, how do we explain this? Obviously the thought isn't the source of their feelings or they would have the exact same sensation when thinking the same thought!"

Some thoughts are so intrinsically part of us we can't see them or recognize them as "Not I's" at all. We see them as truths, like our arms or legs. This is a result of adopting opinions, ideas, or beliefs, so completely that any contrast seems 'wrong' and out of place. Like water is to a fish, we live in the thoughts, breathe and speak through them all day every day, without any awareness of how thoroughly they filter our view and experience of EVERYTHING! Fish think water is all there is, until you take them out of it.

We believe our opinions are us, and we believe we are them. When we aren't! This is just weird! The phenomenon becomes really interesting and obvious when we sit across from someone operating through a completely opposing set of swallowed beliefs and truths. This is the perfect moment to allow and perhaps experience another viewpoint. Why not look through someone else's eyes and life for a second and appreciate how they have constructed their world. We can resist and dig in our heals, or open up, explore, and allow cooperative possibilities to unfold. Simply enjoying differences without judgment would bring lasting progress to humanity!

Unfortunately, there are those of us so convinced with the validity of our thoughts and beliefs that we lose all ability to listen objectively to another perspective being presented. Self-righteous behavior over who holds the best viewpoint is a perscription for failure and misery. To see and cultivate the vast potential on the planet right now we must set aside our need to defend our 'rightness' and make some room for other's to have their opinions and beliefs.

Every choice to allow and gain distance from our repetitive thoughts, recognizing them as "Not I's" brings a profound possibility to merge with the larger part of ourselves and make a connection and a difference with whomever we are with. As we become aware that we are not our individual conditioned ways of thinking and feel the observer behind our ideas, we experience something more valuable than winning or being right. We become peaceful. From this place we intuitively create honoring relationships and operate through kind understanding, knowing that other viewpoints will always exist.

⇌

We are rising above compulsive thinking and by compulsive thinking I mean unconscious thinking that is conditioned by the past. Humanity's destiny now, and it's already happening, is to rise above thinking ... then thinking will have found its place. It will no longer dominate your existence. You are moving, the shift is, from being a predominantly thinking entity with a few lucid moments to being a predominantly aware being ... a shift from thinking to awareness. Awareness is spacious attention.

Eckhart Tolle

⇌

It's the thoughts we hold that delineate the sensations we have. Here is a mind boggling question, "How do you become so seduced by a little string of words? How is it when words are put together in a particular way they create a huge feeling in you?" You can't see the thought. You can't surgically remove it. But you know it's there because you can feel it! Who put it there? How do you let it go? Who would you be without it? Would you like to be more in control of the little rascals (Not I's) that seem to have dominion over your moments! You know when they are dancing around out of control. They're distracting, thwarting, self sabotaging, and critical in nature. They love conflict, superiority, and if you don't Catch & Release them, they always notice what is wrong with life.

Thoughts happen, they always will. The key is to let the non-deliberate yammer of "Not I's" flow right on by. Let the river flow through without resistance. We can get good at observing thoughts providing we don't dissect, analyze, and pick at them like an old wound. Be selective in what you give your attention to and get good at recognizing any habit of criticism, blame, or self doubt that may be running on automatic. Use the Catch & Release process on ideas and compulsive banter. Just as you apply Catch & Release to resistance, apply it to repetitive thinking. You can release the habit of gerbiling (running on a wheel that goes in circles only to stop in the exact location you started from). Notice the feeling, sensation, or idea you are avoiding by this nonstop banter. This is a good one (yes, I've done it myself). Once found, apply the Catch & Release steps and decide, "Releasing repetitive thinking." Deciding is critical. You can let go of anything… providing you own it as your baby.

We must pick which thoughts we will feed. Much like animals, the one's we nourish will grow bigger and stronger. If we give haunting thoughts enough of our life force they become so large they often back us into a corner and become our authority. All the while we are the one's making it so.

There is evidence to support anything we want to believe. Finding some real truth–our own, which exists beyond anything we have been given or taught, inspires us toward our unique and very integral purpose for living.

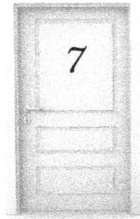

Welcome to Door #7

Let the Story Go

•Apply Catch & Release to any repetitive story or repetitive thoughts you would like to be free of.

Example 1

David has had a consistent internal dialogue about not making as much money as he used to. He catches himself lost in this story a few times a week, blaming the government for his financial predicament. He often repeats his story to a couple of close friends, when they'll listen. He wants to let the negative and blame filled story end. He doesn't feel good when he tells it. It upsets him. Those around him have been affected too. He realizes how discouraging and inhibiting all this resentment and finger pointing is.

He's efficient with Catch & Release now and has learned that the most thorough releases come with total ownership of what he is thinking and feeling. He easily imagines himself repeating the story and then he begins to feel his 'story telling' personality. He felt a lot of righteousness, blame, and superiority creeping in. He noticed his body posture change as he imagined himself telling his resentful tale. He saw his story teller's agenda and it was unpleasant to admit how destructive his intentions were. He wanted to get agreement even if it meant discouraging others and ruining their day. He felt his story telling persona and began to own what it was doing to his life, his family and his health. He deeply felt how much this story was consuming his supply of creative energy for manifesting success. He wanted to be free of it in a hurry. He decided to release it by saying, "Releasing the need to tell this story." He waited, unsure... sensing some anxiety so he went ahead and felt that sensation. He let it be there. He sat with it for a minute and just felt anxt without any resistance. He owned the feeling as his thought, his idea, and his decision. It was interesting because he was very clear the anxiety was not him, but it was his. This experience of tension was very familiar to him and always an element of telling his story. He sat with it, owned it entirely, and decided he was ready to let it go. He declared with certainty, "Releasing the need to tell this story." He felt lighter and really liked this ability to let the whole thing go at once. He decided if the urge came to tell his story, he would catch it before a word left his mouth and apply Catch & Release quickly on the spot. He intended to never tell the story again.

He picked creating wealth as his feeling of choice (you can pick ANY feeling). He imagined himself phoning prospects, attracting clients, being magnetic, helpful, and in demand. He pictured his appointment book full and liked that feeling so much he saturated himself with it. He felt his love for his company and his work and sat in gratitude for a few minutes unexpectedly. (When resistance is cleared, space is opened for our natural state of being... happiness). He felt very comforted, confident and more in charge of his future. This was his favorite Catch & Release so far. He felt different and was determined to have this new feeling of creating success take the place of all his complaining.

Example 2

There was a student in our Principles of Allowing series that discovered she could apply Catch & Release to an entire story with one swoop! She realized she had a tale she had been repeating to herself since she was in the fourth grade when her teacher laughingly told her, "You will never be an artist." She trusted this authority figure and began reciting the "I can't" story to herself from that moment forward. With each invitation to participate in an artistic project she proclaimed the fable's accuracy by sharing the story yet again, to all that would listen. She fed that event a lot of her attention over the years and had plenty of agreement and reinforcement from family. Until that day in class, when at 56 years of age she decided it was time for a new story. She declared this fable and these thoughts were being kept alive by her own doing, she got it! When you genuinely own, you can release. If she blames what she is experiencing on the teacher, she has no power over it, the teacher does.

During class that night she was quiet as she realized the feelings associated with the story were of giving her power away, not believing in herself, and trusting other's opinions over her own. She didn't know this story had become such a part of her. She gently allowed the story to exist for a moment. She felt what it has been like to have this story as part of her life for so long. She let the feelings saturate her senses. She let it be there without resistance and when she was ready she let it go by clearly deciding, "Releasing this story." She decided with all her heart to let it go. She was beaming when she finished, she felt an opening, a possibility that hadn't been there just a few moments before. She realized the old thoughts may wander through her consciousness again but she was confident she could Catch & Release the story until it no longer appeared.

I asked her if she would like to invite in a new idea to fill that space and she closed her eyes as if cruising a buffet of choices and she picked the feeling, "I believe in myself." We all experienced the words as she spoke them. Her decision was palpable. She closed her eyes and let the sensations of believing in herself fill her senses, it filled ours too. We were all very connected… like water to a fish.

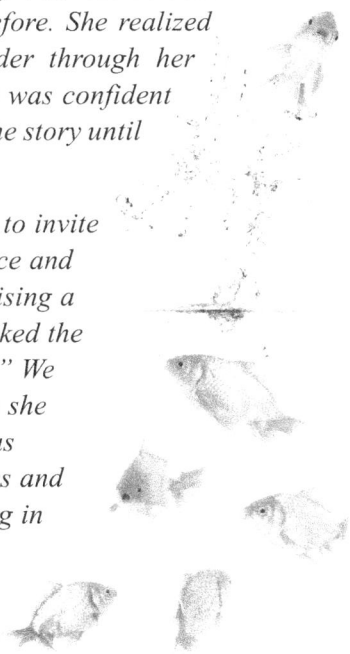

91

✺

You are powerful beyond anything you have believed yourself to be! You are filled with everything it takes to create a life experience you treasure. The energy moving through your body and mind is akin to a beam of light, so bright it gives existence to whatever you point it toward.

This is POWER...

This is YOU!

You have a stream of energy that creates worlds moving through you. This is what you do in every moment of every day... ignite what you focus on.

As you become more aware of your creator beam, you begin to see that every person you encounter has their own. They have a stream, a potent force made of expectation, and it always and forever manifests exactly what it's being pointed at.

When we point our light toward desires, we manifest dreams. When we remind others how to point theirs, we experience profound purpose.

✺

CHAPTER EIGHT

Positive WHAT?

Let's talk about positive thinking for a minute before we go on. Positive thinking is usually adopted as a strategy to resist negative thinking. Positive thinking is frequently an effort to believe something we actually don't believe but wish we did. It's like trying to push a pretty reality on top of an ugly reality we have been avoiding feeling and owning. Positive thinking works for a while, providing we're feeling ambitious, healthy, and had a good night's sleep. We can repeat and restate the new positive thought all day, post it on little notes in the space we hang out in, and reprogram ourselves to memorize it fairly well. Until… our guard is down, we're tired, ill, or emotional. This is when the old reality seems to stick its ugly head right back into our world. It didn't go away. It was just being pushed down by our perky effort to think something on top of it, over it, and instead of it.

Have you ever noticed how that old habit or pain is still there ready to be activated when you're not on your toes? IT HAS TO BE EXPERIENCED TO BE RELEASED! It is so much easier to feel a resisted feeling for a bit and let it go, than it is to try and think positive on top of it, through it, or with it always there looming in the background.

Positive thinking isn't a bad thing. A hopeful thought definitely feels better than a negative monologue. It certainly offers a few minutes of relief to change our focus from a painful thought over to an idea such as, *everything works out perfectly!* I just don't see positive thinking as the most efficient path to create any lasting change. Besides, positive thinking has become such a fad it implies negative thinking should be resisted, and at the very least not admitted! Most people try to hide their negative talk and negative feelings like they are wrong or bad for having them. Now that we are surrounded by the 'Think Positive Police,' our pretending to be positive has actually resulted in more resistance to what we truly feel!

Positive believing would be a fad worth creating! How to believe in something is a skill worth exploring. Believing includes genuine heartfelt knowing that something IS! Believing means something is truly felt without doubts and fears. No pretending. When we believe something we operate through it, we become it. No pretense, no stacking a smile on top of a pain or forcing a happy thought on top of a hurtful discouraging one. Positive believing would be the real deal!

How do we create a genuine feeling?

We decide to! With all the intention we can muster. We choose and manifest this idea, sensation, and feeling that we long to experience. We imagine it, bathe in it, see it in our lives, and cultivate the sensations of it with all our heart. We do this for however long it takes for this experience to become ours. We commit to apply Catch & Release to any story of 'can't,' or 'won't,' so we don't stack this newly desired feeling on top of old resistant thoughts, ideas, and sensations (which will keep attracting the reality of their negative vibration). We implement this strategy of Catch & Release until true conviction pulses through our veins with excitement.

You know you are making progress by how you feel. You sense the new idea coming to life with each effort to cultivate it. You continue to eliminate any interference and it keeps growing. You feel how your focus on it is giving it life and you begin to trust your ability to manifest your own experience. This new vibration in you begins to act as a magnet to reality, automatically bringing you more of the same. Why is it working? Because you chose the feeling you wanted to feel, YOU decided! And, YOU are excited about making it real! Passion creates reality! When you cultivate a feeling from authentic hungry desire and eliminate any blocks and obstacles of doubt, you WILL manifest your desire. Now this would grow some positive believing into a sensational existence!

꿈꿈

The thoughts that you think, regarding those things that you want, set into motion the creation, and eventual fulfillment, of that which you want. And likewise, the thoughts that you think, regarding those things that you do not want, set into motion the creation, and eventual fulfillment, of that which you do NOT want.

The thoughts that you set forth in combination with great emotion are the most powerful of your thoughts.

Abraham-Hicks

Having a genuine positive outlook and developing a skill of appreciating what is wonderful in the world is a practice worth adopting. If… while intending to notice and enjoy the magical reality around you, you become emotional or resistant, look the distraction in the eye for a second and say hello. Watch the unsettling idea melt with your pure attention to it. The interruption showing up is a gift, making its self known in that red hot moment so you can finally let it go. Sometimes when we put our attention toward a reality we want to manifest old blocks and habits will show up. No worries! This is cause for celebration. Each resistant response you Catch offers a grand opportunity to gather up your precious creative energy so you can redirect it into dreams.

Welcome to Door #8

Stop Pretending

•List anything you have been trying to be positive about, but really aren't.

•Apply Catch & Release to doubts, fears, and obstacles and passionately choose the idea, feeling, or sensation you decide to make real in their place.

Example

Sally has been trying to be positive about her health but underneath her positive affirmations she has been very afraid of what might be wrong. She has been suffering with abdominal pain accompanied by lower back pain. She feared it was something serious but kept repeating and trying to think good thoughts like, "I am healthy, I will be okay, and I can do this." After reading this chapter she realized she was trying really hard to believe these thoughts, but something was in the way. She was eager to eliminate the obstacles and see if this would help. She immediately went to the question, "What feeling do I NOT want to have?" The answer was right in front of her.

She didn't want to be sick. She was afraid of cancer getting her, like it had her best friend. She wasn't just a little scared. The suffering of her friend was very frightening and close to her. Even though her heart was already beating fast and nervousness had flooded her senses, she was aware this pool of resistance was not her. This alarming feeling was a "Not I" and with this understanding came confidence and acceptance. She was ready to let go of this dread-full feeling. Sally willingly breathed in the sensations of her fear of cancer, the resistance, the pushing, the avoiding, the denying… and surrendered. She let her resistance to cancer consume her for a few minutes, even trembling for a few seconds. A very present part of her seemed to be with her, watching, alert. She felt comforted by this and continued. She breathed in her resistance to cancer and felt the truth of it deep in her bones. She let her fear exist. She acknowledged it, experienced it, allowed it, and finally she owned it. It was absolutely hers.

Experiencing the sensations didn't take as long as she thought. The disturbing feeling began to lessen and diminish with her determination to allow it. Quietness filled her. She sat still, almost grateful, realizing this terror was not her but something she had been lugging around and making more real with her inability to admit it. She exhaled deeply and released the collection of feelings very deliberately by clearly deciding, "Releasing resistance to cancer." She felt the ideas and fear flow out of her body, leave, and trickle into nothingness. It was astounding. She had put so much effort into not feeling that horror she was speechless, soft, and thankful to be free. She clearly felt relief from fear. She understood how not owning and releasing her resistance to being sick acted as a magnet to ill-health. She made a note to apply this to the sensations in her body that she had been ignoring. She knew letting go of her resistance to the pain would allow her to begin healing.

She finished up her Catch & Release session by contemplating, "What experience do I treasure? What feeling am I passionate to cultivate in my life right now? What can I really get into and flow my heart and horsepower toward authentically?" She thought for a minute and then selected, being willing to feel... being willing to feel WHATEVER... ALLOWING! She laughed at how simple allowing could be compared to resisting. She was thrilled with the idea of going through life with such openness, without fear of a feeling as though a feeling could harm her. She imagined who she would be if she were allowing in her relationships, with her daughter, with her body. Wow. She closed her eyes and took some time to picture going through her day experiencing what was in front of her instead of avoiding it; it was relaxing and filled with ease. She visualized the events of her day moving through her like her breath. She could breath in a sensation, allow it, and breathe it out. It felt so open, so opposite from the closed feeling she has experienced most of her life. She felt great satisfaction and pleasure with her choice.

Sally cultivated this lovely sensation of allowing for the rest of her day. She was very content.

my angel, my mother

～

There is an ever present pool of energy available for you to direct toward dreams. Some refer to it as a host of beings, many label them angels... some prefer to call it mom or dad, and many term the sacredness God. This divine intelligence is with you every moment you allow it to be. It waits for you to beckon its presence so it can assist you in igniting and creating dreams and desires.

When your call to the invisible is birthed from passionate longing, with a strong belief in its presence, miracles abound.

You are a GIFT

You are a gift to the matrix and with each wish you add delight to the sea of possibility that holds us all! Want with all your heart and ask with the fire of a dreamer! This exciting flow of energy can only be reflected back to you in the form of possibility.

～

CHAPTER NINE

Victim HOOD

This is not a beat yourself up chapter, this is a celebrate ownership and change debilitating patterns opportunity! Give yourself lots of room to allow and notice whatever responses may be triggered in you from this reading. Take a deep breath and feel the part of you that would genuinely like to know yourself better.

Language is very important. Every thought you think has a specific sensation, every intention you hold has a specific vibration. How you speak influences the reality you will be experiencing next. Think grieving thoughts and you will become sad, think thoughts of happiness and you will become more joyful, think thoughts of "I can't," and you are immediately limited. "Can't" is the mantra of a victim.

*Experience the difference between these two statements by filling in the blank with a feeling you have difficulty managing, i.e., frustration, anger, sadness, blame, laziness, victimhood, etc.

• Sometimes I can let go of my _____ and sometimes I can't.

• Sometimes I can let go of my _____ and sometimes I won't. *(Fill in the blank with the same feeling)*

Notice how you feel with each statement. One creates ownership of your experience, the other proclaims victimhood.

*Borrowed from Kayt Campbell author of: *Me, not Me – Living the Difference Between Who We Are and What We're Not.*

෴

Watch your thoughts, for they become words.

Choose your words, for they become actions.

Understand your actions, for they become habits.

Study your habits, for they will become your character.

Develop your character, for it becomes your destiny.

Author Unknown

෴

Our mission should we choose to accept it, is to pay closer attention to what we are emitting into the world via our thinking, feeling, and intending. Owning what we discover within ourselves is the true path to freedom because the world will always reflect our inner most selves back to us. Without fail, without falter, every moment of every day we're solely in charge of what we flow into our environment. Whether it is deliberate or on automatic, it is ours. We like to blame circumstances, superiors, government, rules and regulations, and even God for what we attract. When it comes to patterns that are repeating regarding abundance, relationship or well being, it is our own energy returning to us. We are more in charge of what we are experiencing in life than we believe.

This can be hard to grasp for several reasons. One is, we often have reactions and responses to the world that we do not reveal or express TO ANYONE! We basically pretend they don't exist so thoroughly that we can't see them without a searchlight and a strong dose of honesty, and even then it can be difficult. Not admitting or owning our secrets makes it hard to understand how our environment could possibly be reflecting these hidden thoughts, feelings, and intentions when we haven't even disclosed them to ourselves. We seldom share our critical, ornery, or punishing intentions freely. We push them down and label them wrong and unsuitable for revealing. Unfortunately or fortunately (it all depends on how you look at it) those nasty monologues, criticisms, and resentments, no matter how brief or denied, are still right there doing what vibrations do... beckoning similar energy and attracting people and experiences that will match. It is a strange phenomenon but I am sure you will find it reliable upon investigation. Our vibration is a beacon we need to become aware of, disclosed or not.

We can think positive over top of what is churning deep inside and many of us do this, but our innermost beliefs and feelings leak through pretense and invite more of themselves to the party.

The repeating scenarios we draw toward us in present time may not exactly match the incidents of the past, at least not to the T. The situations may be quite diverse in nature and appearance. However, they are usually of the same genre in sensation. For example, betrayal, abuse, dishonesty, or pretense, might be an act we accuse others of, yet upon further scrutiny we discover it is specifically what we're carrying forward from the past. With one exception, we were on the other side of the equation. We were the abuser; we were the betrayer or abandoner. If we sincerely reflect, we usually find there's someone out there who believes we have used, hurt, manipulated, or betrayed them just as we are saying someone is behaving toward us right now. As we become more honest about what, who, and how we may have engaged others in our past we typically find we've hurt another in a manner similar to what we are currently complaining about as a victim. This can be an interesting and humbling exploration! The bottom line is this, quite often the reality coming back toward us is one we previously delivered to someone else…it's merely wearing a different face. What we're not admitting and owning on the inside is usually related to what we attract, observe, and resist on the outside. The feelings match more accurately than the circumstances.

You may feel like you should turn the page quickly on this chapter, confirming inwardly that this information doesn't apply to you. You may oppose the idea that you have anything to do with what you are attracting into your life. I understand. Bad things happen, disasters strike, tragedy is real and loss can break our hearts into tiny little pieces and we prefer to believe that we had nothing to do with any kind of hurt. *I am not saying to look at the horror of an event such as this and find where you have inflicted this type of pain on another. Unless you believe

If you are suffering a tragedy there is one thing you can do that will bring small doses of relief. Feel the pain on purpose. Decide to feel it. This may seem strange but this is the only effective path to relief I have witnessed. Resisting or blaming someone, self included, makes recovery more difficult and severe. Apply Catch & Release and have someone hold you often. Continue surrendering to the pain that is present, feel it, as much as you can allow, then release. Repeat all the above for as long as it takes to see a wisp of silver lining. There is one… understandably it can take time for your heart to recognize it.

it's worth a look. Remember, this is not a beat yourself up chapter! This is a 'take ownership' of the experience of life you are having and resisting. This is an opportunity for lasting change. The feelings, ideas, and sensations that keep repeating are your clues.

Once we recognize and own our past behaviors we can end repeating scenarios, and move on. If we continue to deny behaviors and not forgive ourselves or another we continue to draw similar events, relationships, and circumstances until we release the old vibration.

Do you have a repetitive experience of losing deals, being betrayed, or attracting unfaithful clients and friends? Are you accused of wrong doings you haven't committed? Are you unfairly treated by someone you care about? If so, this is the perfect time to question if you've behaved in a similar fashion to your abuser... at some point in your life. Simply exploring for a moment and discovering where you may have accused, blamed, or hurt someone in the same way you're feeling betrayed right now is time well spent. Once you discover a situation where you behaved poorly and you willingly experience what that other person must have felt like on the receiving end of your abuse, situations transform. Ownership of the similarity dissolves the blame you are feeling and frees up a tremendous surge of creative energy. The willingness to admit and experience a past mistake and comprehend the pain you may have caused another dismantles the repeating pattern you're now attracting. Catch & Release fully applies to any sensations denied, resisted, or blamed... always and forever.

We aren't bad people and we aren't alone, we just made a few mistakes we failed to admit and handle along the way. Do you know anyone who hasn't made mistakes? We are human beings, learning, growing, and discovering. Let's give each other a little growing room. Mistakes happen.

⤙⤚

A man should never be ashamed to own he has been in the wrong, which is but saying... that he is wiser today than he was yesterday.

Alexander Pope

⤙⤚

Don't make this a heavy undertaking! We're all learning to assume more responsibility for what is happening in our lives, more than ever before on planet Earth. As Byron Katie says, "When we know better, we do better." This is a wonderful thing. Hat's off to anyone ready to take more ownership of where they find themselves right now.

What we attract is a reflection, showing us to ourselves. This can be good news or discouraging news, depending on how you look at it. Many consider this grace. The good news comes from allowing what is flowing toward us to be a reminder, a golden opportunity to check in and feel what our innermost intentions might be brewing. This is valuable information to guide us in restructuring and becoming more responsible for any hidden motivation(s) that might not be admitted or shared with partners, co-workers, or family. When we are pretending to want one thing but truly desire another, accomplishment will always be filled with struggle. Intentions secretly moving in misaligned directions create havoc and confusion for all concerned. As we become more honest and reveal our innermost intentions an energetic phenomenon occurs almost instantly, life lines up with us. Goals that have been difficult flow into place and a very real care for others develops. We take responsibility for how we have wasted the creative energy of those near us, by not being honest.

Becoming more real about who we are and what we want is a powerful undertaking for eliminating self sabotage patterns. As we admit, own, and forgive, we intuitively begin to move forward, intending that our actions benefit others. When we operate with care for those walking beside us satisfaction and wealth are the natural result. Taking responsibility for what is moving toward us gives us access to our most powerful self. We become manifesting machines!

The notion that what is flowing toward us is actually coming from us can seem like very bad news if we're smack dab in the middle of feeling like a victim. A victim personality thrives on bad news. A victim can rattle off evidence for how wrong, no good, guilty, and worthless something is in mere seconds. A victim personality might cleverly try to add this perspective of the world reflecting us into their "I am a bad person" file. Or perhaps the author of this chapter will go into their "crazy person" file. Or perhaps there is an "I didn't mean to do it" file. That's all okay! They're all in the same filing cabinet in the same drawer, under the victim category. Don't fall into this drawer and waste your life!

There is a huge opportunity in exploring the notion of being a victim. Having the courage to investigate the nature of any victim personality or behavior can manifest a change of great magnitude in life. With perseverance and ownership of any hopeless victim tendency a new space in the filing cabinet will appear … for joy!

How do I know so much about this subject? I was the number one victim on planet earth (in my mind). I competed for that prize, proved the truth of it, and collected my winnings. Unfortunately my pot of gold at the end of the rainbow was filled with self inflicted pain and suffering. Oh, I got to be right about being treated unfairly, and I proved it repeatedly by failing, feeling miserable, and blaming it all on my parents and my past. Hooray! I won! Sadly, I destroyed my body and my spirit in the process. I was vengefully determined to make sure everyone knew I was abused and betrayed and added more misery with every telling of my story. I never took responsibility for what I felt or how broken my heart was and as long as I blamed what I was feeling on someone outside of me, I wasn't in charge of changing it. I tried to suffer enough to get an apology that never came. I wanted restitution, I wanted blood… and until I got it, I was sworn to suffering.

A victim loves being right about others being wrong and very often will do whatever it takes to prove this, including endure severe pain, be it consciously or not. I failed at my health, at love, and tried to have money soothe my wounds (impossible for very long). The really twisted thing is that part of me felt successful by proving how wrong my parents, society, and even God was. This is the ultimate self sabotage, winning by failing. My being horribly ill and unhappy was how I punished my parents. That's insanity. Guess who I ended up punishing.

I was an extreme case. Mostly people just want to rest, have a break and not have to work so hard for a little happiness. Being a victim can feel like a form of relief from responsibility, a nap of sorts, a little get away. Sometimes becoming sick or broken for a while gives us a hall pass, freedom from having to perform, etc. Careful though, it doesn't feel satisfying for very long and it can become one of those patterns we stick in the back closet, forget about, and then attract from others. If you are surrounded by people who can't be relied upon to take responsibility, well...

If you experience unjust behavior or deception on your path to success, take heart, this is not a bad thing. This is merely an indication you may have some sneaky intentions somewhere in the mix of your life. Maybe not in the exact arena they seem to be coming from. It could involve a different person from another time. Maybe from an incident in the past where you or another made a mistake and you haven't forgiven it. The obstacle you are now hitting brings a very important opening. Thank goodness it is finally showing up so you can release the annoying pattern and recover the creative energy it has been stealing. Consider the perfection of it showing up, here, now, at this point in your life. You must be ready to let it go or it wouldn't be knocking on your door. Truly, this discovery is a blessing so we can be free of our need to punish one another and add something more valuable and lasting to the world.

The humility that comes with every drop of ownership gives birth to a more compassionate and loving awareness in our dealings with others. We begin to realize that what most suffer from isn't the wrong doings of perpetrators as much as it is a feeling of fear, anger, or non-forgiveness that keeps vibrating from our past and attracting circumstances to prove its correctness. We start to understand that a new way to be kind to those we love is to gently guide them to retract the finger they are pointing outward and invite them to discover how they may be attracting the very experience(s) they keep feeling limited by.

As I catch myself blaming another, if I'm on my toes, a smile often crosses my face as I recognize what's really happening. I instantly look for how I may have committed the very act I am blaming or accusing another for. Then, I grow appreciation for THEM showing me to myself! Sometimes I wonder if this lovely trigger wasn't the perfect rendezvous (yes this realization usually arrives after a few rounds of Catch & Release). Maybe it was all orchestrated by my higher self or divine intelligence, maybe the whole drama was a plan from long ago - an old agreement - a contract of sorts, and maybe they were just keeping their end of the deal.

Playing their role to remind me to wake up and become Source of my experience of being human. You decide how far you let this one in…

I have some exciting news! This beaconing phenomenon works both ways and once we begin to embrace that what we flow out flows back, we naturally cultivate the determination to be more responsible for what we feel, think, and intend. Reality becomes our greatest teacher and friend, honestly showing us to ourselves. As we increasingly understand that what is coming toward us is merely a reflection, our experience of life gets really fun. Blame becomes an experience of the past and health is often restored. Responsibility is the true path to freedom.

⤚⤚

You are the creator of your own life experience, and as the creator of your experience, it is important to understand that it is not by virtue of your action, not by virtue of your doing, it is not even by virtue of what you are saying that you are creating. You are creating by virtue of the vibration that you are offering.

Abraham-Hicks

⤚⤚

Welcome to Door #9

Response Ability

•What feeling or experience are you having in life that is not your fault?

•List your spontaneous answer(s). Include any feelings, sensations, or ideas triggered by reading this chapter. Apply Catch & Release. If you would rather pull weeds or quickly move on to the next chapter you might ask what feeling you are NOT wanting to have right now.

Example

David listed, people repeatedly schedule appointments to meet with me and then cancel and never reschedule, without ever giving a valid reason why. This is not any doing of mine, I make myself very available.

I don't like the idea that people are sick and suffering from disease of their own doing. I don't agree that we are attracting our experience. I think some people have traumatic things happen in their life by no doing or thinking of their own. I feel irritated by this chapter.

I just realized I am blaming how I feel on what I just read when it is MY response to what I read that I am feeling. I do know how I feel right now is coming from inside of me, from my opinions and beliefs. I will Catch & Release this feeling of irritation before I continue.

David began... "I am irritated. What feeling am I not wanting to have? Uncertainty. I don't like not knowing what I am attracting and I am not sure I totally agree with you about me attracting it. Let me ask again, What am I avoiding feeling? I know what it is, not knowing! I despise not knowing. I need to release this frustrated and very agitated feeling."

David took a couple of breaths, this helped in the past when he was over-thinking or over-analyzing which blocked his ability to feel. He tried to relax and sat back in his chair, he even closed his eyes for a minute trying to calm his mind down. He felt pressure and resistance, he was extremely uncomfortable. He thought to himself this is a big one. I had no idea how much I resisted Not Knowing! He took a couple more breaths and tried to relax, and repeated to himself, "Allow the feelings David. Allow them! They can't leave unless you feel them for a minute." This helped him settle down and become more willing. He knew it was true and he definitely wanted them gone. He reminded himself to open up and breathe in the discomfort.

David realized he needed to let go of his resistance to the idea of not knowing! His resistance to the feeling was strong and overwhelming. Just feeling his resistance really helped. This was where he was. This was the feeling he was sitting in. He dropped into how much he despised this idea of "Not Knowing." He just let his resistance be there, he felt it, he looked it in the eye, and even noticed it in his chest area like a weight, and he felt tremendous anxiety. He kept breathing into his resistance to "Not Knowing" and let all the sensations be there. He finally began to calm down and was able to allow it all. As he relaxed a little more he felt a sensation of sadness. He let it be there for a minute. It reminded him of when he was a child and felt like he was going to get in trouble for not doing well enough in school. It was all part of this resistance to "Not Knowing". He felt all the feelings, he couldn't help it, they were there. He sat quietly amazed at how strong his resistance was and how adamantly opposed he was to "Not Knowing." He saw how this has been a thread through his entire life, resisting "Not Knowing." He was finally able to feel the fear he had carried forward from so long ago. He owned it as his feeling. He totally accepted that this was his collection of ideas and sensations. He was ready to let them go. He stated with a strong sense of deciding, "Releasing resistance to Not Knowing." He lingered in the feeling of letting it go and really felt the freedom of deciding to release resistance. Again, he understood the tremendous value in deciding. He realized now that his resistance to the feeling was gone, he was ready to feel the feeling he had been resisting. He went for it! He invited the feeling of "Not Knowing" and it was right there. He could feel his turmoil, fear, shame, and many other emotions that accompanied the idea of "Not Knowing" and he continued the process and the release.

David had a few insights, the first being he couldn't feel something if he was resisting it. He couldn't get into the feeling until he let go of his resistance to feeling it. The second insight was that "Not Knowing" was the cause of him suffering over the cancelled appointments. He didn't mind if they cancelled, he hated not knowing why! He planned to continue Catching & Releasing the ideas connected to this discovery when he had more time. The third insight was having a sense of how his resistance was like a magnet attracting people to cancel; he had an intuitive feeling that this was a reflection of his inner state. It had been happening his whole life and in a strange way he understood it was something he was attracting with his hate of it. His fear of it actually kept it very alive in his vibration. He had many friends that never had any issue with this phenomenon; they were definitely vibrating and attracting a different reality than he was.

He wondered what feeling would change what he was drawing toward him. He thought about it for a minute and came up with the feeling of being valuable. He liked that idea. He recalled a time when his wife was very grateful for how hard he worked. He invited in that sense of being valued. He imagined it and brought the feeling into the present moment. He really enjoyed the sensation. He liked creating a feeling he chose instead of spending a lifetime resisting one he despised. He looked around his office, felt his value, breathed it in, allowed it to fill his senses and was very excited to share this discovery with his wife. He thought she probably had some idea of it all along.

≈≈

Behold
GOODNESS

What you are living is the evidence of what you are thinking and feeling, every single time.

By choosing better feeling thoughts and by speaking more of what you do want and less of what you don't want, you will gently tune yourself to the vibrational frequency of your Broader Perspective. To see your world through the eyes of Source is truly the most spectacular view of life, for from that vibrational vantage point, you are in alignment with, and therefore in the process of attracting, only what you would consider to be the very best of your world.

Abraham-Hicks

≈≈

CHAPTER TEN

Blame Anyone?

Every time we point at someone in an effort to blame them for what we are going through, notice… one finger is pointing at them but three are pointing back toward us. This is not easy to see from certain viewpoints or during particular times of life, understandably so.

This may help…

As long as you blame someone or something for what you are feeling then something outside of you has to change so you can feel better.

As long as you blame a past event for what you are experiencing in the present, you are giving the old event power over the moment you are in right now.

As long as you blame the government for your production or income levels, you're giving them power over your ability to manifest.

If you repeatedly blame a parent for how your life is turning out, you often keep failing or suffering to prove you are right about them being wrong.

As long as you blame the weather for your response to life, you have to wait for the weather to improve so you can have a different response.

If you blame being betrayed in the past for your unwillingness to connect or be intimate with another now, you have not owned that your feelings come from inside of you.

If you are blaming the actions or non-actions of someone for how you feel physically, you are putting your health in the hands of others.

If you blame someone you work with for driving you crazy, it's you who has given them the steering wheel.

If you blame someone who passed away for your loneliness, you are holding them responsible for your suffering.

If you are angry at someone and have been unwilling to forgive, you are handing them your happiness.

If you are blaming yourself for a past mistake, you may be unconsciously punishing yourself by making decisions and attracting relationships that insure your continued suffering.

Blaming ourselves repeatedly for mistakes has no value and sabotages resolution, prosperity, and health. Assuming full responsibility for mistakes and not repeating them is knowledge applied. Knowledge applied is wisdom.

If you are blaming your new shoes for your feet hurting, change your shoes.

The moment we take responsibility for what we are feeling is the moment our life circumstances begin to change.

Whatever degree we are willing to own what we feel is the exact degree we will be able to change it.

Whatever degree we blame what we feel on something or someone else is the exact degree we will be un-able to change it.

Ready to recover your creative energy?

Welcome to Door #10

Freedom From Blame

•Make a list of anyone or anything you are blaming for how you feel.

• To experience profound freedom apply Catch & Release to each item on your list.

Example 1

David listed his father for not showing him affection, and his broker for the money he lost in the stock market. He didn't know who to blame for gas prices, but he was constantly researching the matter. He also listed his wife for not being more intimate more often, his ex-wife for her unjustifiable greed, and he had to admit he was blaming God the almighty for the chaotic turmoil in the world.

David was curious what this exercise would reveal. He chose blaming his broker to start with because it was weighing on him. He settled into his question, "What feeling am I not wanting to feel by blaming him for my loss?" He sat there, stewing in a bit of resentment and asked again, "What feeling am I avoiding?" There it was, quick and ugly, "I should've known!" It hit him like a slap in the face. This was on the same thread as his last few Catch & Releases. His face felt hot, he felt the pang of it immediately. He was avoiding the feeling that he should have known and prevented the loss. He should have been more responsible. He realized under it all he really was blaming himself and blaming the stock broker allowed him to avoid feeling like he had made a mistake. He sunk in his chair and invited in this feeling, "I should've known." It was right there. He took a minute and felt very disappointed with himself, he felt like a failure, like he had let his family down. He then realized he had been working like a horse trying to pay for his mistake... and this was hurting his family even more. He quieted down and just felt the idea, "I should've known," he realized he's had this self blame in his life since he was a young boy. It was an old familiar sensation. He very determinedly invited the blame in and sat in the sensations for a couple of minutes. He felt the weight of the idea and how it consumed so much of his energy. He let it be there, stay there, and saw its entanglement into many aspects of his life. He felt it completely and owned it as his. He was ready and stated with great conviction, "Releasing the idea, I should've known." He took a deep breath and visualized the feeling moving all the way out of his consciousness... he felt relieved, an empty space is how he described it. Open, willing, unafraid. It was good.

He chose "trusting himself" for the feeling he wanted to experience from now on in his life. This was interesting and very different for him. He had to imagine how it would feel to not worry at work, at home, with the government, or with anything. He wanted to trust himself so completely that his faith superseded his doubt. He imagined living like this, and it was very calming, very relaxing as he allowed the sensation to be born. It was coming, he could feel it... he repeated it a couple of times... "Trust in life, trust in my choices, trust in what is coming, trust, trusting myself... hmmm." Trust was flowing in and it was a comforting new sensation, one he planned to choose often.

Example 2

Sally listed herself first and foremost. She blamed herself for not being more together and peaceful after all the courses and money she'd spent to be enlightened. She also secretly blamed her family for not appreciating her more, and her sister for abandoning her. She blamed humanity for what they were doing to the Earth with consumption and waste, Hitler for unspeakable cruelty, and the government for the economic disaster her country was facing.

Sally desperately wanted to release self-blame. She felt relief from just admitting how she'd been blaming herself most of her life. She realized she was in a constant state of discouragement from her habit of self-criticism and that she hardly ever noticed anything good about herself. Her clarity of how blame was sabotaging her life was both good and bad mixed together. She was glad to see the pattern, but also disappointed in herself. She realized that exact idea, being disappointed, was finger pointing and was just more of the same. She wasn't going to get sidetracked.

She took a deep breath and said to herself, "Going in!" She relaxed and became quiet minded for a few minutes before questioning herself, "What feeling, idea, or sensation am I avoiding by blaming?" After a few minutes of silence a word popped into her mind and it was very strange indeed. The word was joy. She didn't get it at first... she pondered... "avoiding joy?" It took her a minute to wrap her mind and heart around this idea but she did realize joy was a feeling she often denied. She became very still. Confused but relentless, she kept feeling her way to more clarity. She stayed present and waited, she didn't push. She knew she was on to something. She took a deep breath and felt the idea of resisting joy. It was very familiar and automatic to not let herself have that feeling. A very sad sensation enveloped her, she allowed it and kept feeling it until she understood. She resisted feeling joy because she knew it wouldn't last, that someone would take it from her in a cruel way and it would hurt too much to allow. To not feel joy was safer. To feel joy ended up in pain. To stay in suffering was how she tried to avoid having to suffer by surprise.

Sally dropped into a pool of deep sorrow. She stayed in the feeling until she could allow it with zero resistance. It finally lessened. She became acutely aware. She felt her fear of joy. Sally actually observed several incidents where she avoided the feeling by keeping herself busy. She had never let herself get too close to it. She experienced this thoroughly. This behavior had defined her for a very long time. She began to realize this was a choice, an old choice, a crazy one, and she understood she could let it go now, because she decided to. Strangely, she felt as though she was getting ready to say goodbye to a very old companion. She proclaimed, "Releasing my resistance to joy." It was as if a dark cloud left her body. She felt it dissolving and gratefully imagined it moving into the earth. She used her hand, making a motion of dismissal from the top of her head all the way to her feet. It was like she was instructing her brain, bones, and tissue to let it all go. It was a powerful release.

She picked "joy" to fill herself back up with. It was surprisingly easy and beautiful. She let the sensation fill her senses to the brim. She delighted herself with it like a child would play in a bath tub with bubbles. She hadn't felt this alive in a very long time. She was full and with each breath she imagined more joy flowing in. She remembered it was okay to be happy, that it was a choice she could make unafraid of future pain. She was at home in herself for the first time in a long while.

∾

There is only one way to make a difference in the lives of others...

BE the example.

Deeply, truly, and gratefully take responsibility for your experience of life. Show others how to be fully responsible for where they place their energy and attention, by being fully responsible for where you place yours.

And... believe in them.

∾

CHAPTER ELEVEN

Criticism - OUCH!

What you look at - you become. What you give your energy and attention to grows. How you habitually view reality creates your experience of life. Noticing what's good, noticing what's bad, noticing what's wrong, noticing what's right, it's all a choice.

What do you spend the majority of your attention focusing on regarding your partner, your family, work, home, weather, war, or in the mirror? Do you notice the wonderment or the un-wonderful? What reality are you investing the majority of your powerful creative energy into?

If you spend a lot of your precious attention on judging, ridiculing, or making yourself or another wrong, you're probably expecting and receiving some type of return for your investment? Otherwise you wouldn't do it! What is it you're wanting in exchange for all the fertilizer you're feeding the unwanted? What is the prize for investing in gossip or being critical of another person?

Do you get some attention, kinship, maybe approval or acceptance? Do you get to somehow win or fit in? Are you punishing a person when you speak negatively about them, perhaps feeling a tad superior when you do? Or, do you get to feel right as you prove someone else to be wrong? Maybe you get to feel like an extra good person each time you point out the bad guys? Heck, if that were true, we should all be feeling like Saints by now!

≈

The need to criticize simply belies a longing for recognition, appreciation, and validation. None of which, however, can be obtained through criticism.

Mike Dooley
Leveraging the Universe:
7 Steps to Engaging Life's Magic

≈

If you put yourself down frequently... are you your own target? What is the pay off for continual self abnegation, for making yourself wrong, and flowing your creative energy in a self destructive way? There has to be something we get from it? I wonder sometimes if convincing ourselves we are not good enough means we finally get to give up, stop working so hard, and take a break from it all. As though not being good enough justifies quitting. Wouldn't it be great if we allowed resting and relaxing without having to pay for it by suffering or hurting enough to deserve it?

Habitually focusing on what is wrong with life, our self, government, earth, or others is a crazy investment with a very bad return since we always get more of what we give. It doesn't feel good, it doesn't produce solutions and we often try to include others in our misery. What is the point? *Note: This is a habitually critical dialogue, not the same as a deliberate intention to discover obstacles and create solutions.*

What we flow out is what we invite the universe to give us back. Chronically noticing what is wrong, and having it as the handy dandy conversation piece when hanging out with family, friends, and strangers in elevators is a good definition of insanity. We talk about what is wrong way more than we share what is right. When visiting or making conversation what do we bring into the moment? What are we adding to the lives of those we touch? What are we making more real in our relationships? What are we eager to share with others?

"Horrible weather isn't it?"

≈≈

When you are complaining, you become a living, breathing crap magnet.

Harv Eker, Secrets of the Millionaire Mind

≈≈

Let's dab our paintbrushes in some new colors...

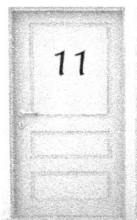

Welcome to Door #11

Notice the Good

• Take two minutes and notice the profundity of life, in people, architecture, smiles, friends, family, stars, the vast sky, waving trees, dancing clouds, your arms, legs, hands, a stone, and the eyes to see it all.

• Repeat step one often - for the rest of your life.

≈≈

Believe

The greatest gift you could ever give another is your unwavering belief in them. As you look into their eyes feel the powerful inner being, speak to this aspect of them, and acknowledge the designer sitting in front of you!

The more we honor another's ability to decide, the more it appears. The more we decide for another and try to control them, the less it appears.

Believe in people... for the most enjoyable and fulfilling ride through life see the best in everyone...self included!

≈≈

CHAPTER TWELVE

YOU

How you treat yourself is an invitation for the world to treat you the same way. You are the display model, the instruction booklet, and the silent instructor to everyone around you... whether you know them or not. People unconsciously and enigmatically mimic the flow of energy we have toward ourselves. They duplicate and travel the attention path we carve out with our thoughts, ideas, and vibrations. If we secretly criticize or privately beat ourselves up, dramatizing where we're sub-par, others unconsciously chime in. If we feign confidence or try to push certainty into place when it just isn't there, reality will match the underlying truth, not the asserted lie. There is a mix of intentions going on all the time, and results can be unpredictable. The more honest we are within ourselves the easier it is to see how the reality inside and the reality outside line up. Vibration and thought attract their match, we vibrate and life responds. Knowing ourselves becomes a priority.

If you honor the learning process you are in, with patience and kindness, allowing your mistakes to help you become more responsible, I bet the world is treating you in a similarly respectful way. If you never feel like you do quite enough, rarely see the good in the mirror, and focus a lot of your attention toward what you don't like about yourself, well... is the world copying you? It is worth an honest look. Really, how is life treating you?

For example, when I get down on myself it is usually over my desire for someone's approval. I can be a bit of an attention monger. I probably should have received the 'great pretender' award somewhere along the line for my skill level at behaving however I needed to behave so someone would attend to me. The result was living with the feeling that nobody genuinely cared about or understood me. Duh, how can anyone understand or create intimacy with a pretender!

The sad news is, if we pretend it means we must be resisting or denying who we really are. When we pretend aren't we are determined to hide our true self? My dad used to say, "If you want to know what you really believe about yourself look at who you're attracting." I didn't like that idea much, but it happened to be spot on. I was a magnet to people who were NOT committed to a caring relationship and who didn't really desire knowing or sharing my innermost dreams. Another duh, I was pretending to be committed to a relationship with me and I didn't even take time to discover my innermost dreams!

A man is a method, a progressive arrangement; a selecting principle, gathering his like to him; wherever he goes.

Ralph Waldo Emerson

If you are attracting relationships that don't work... take a look, are you resisting anything about yourself? Are you forever noticing what's wrong when you look in the mirror? How about when you reflect on your day, do you linger in the moments that were successful and wonderful or focus on upsets and moments you felt unsuccessful? Do you give yourself any credit?

How do you feel about who you are in life right now? How do you like who you have become? How do you treat yourself? Not how you may pretend to treat yourself or how you may pretend to care about yourself in front of others. The question is, how do you truly feel about yourself when you're alone? *No making yourself wrong with this exploration. This is an honest inquiry to reveal what you sincerely experience regarding yourself.*

The first step in creating change is to be very honest about where you are. If you say you like yourself, are you being sincere? If you don't like who you have become it's a good time to start admitting how you focus your attention and energy on the subject of 'you.' It is useful to become aware of your signature method of resisting the reflection in the mirror (or in your mind for those who refrain from mirrors). We all fall into self critical pits now and then. Its okay, we're human. The key is recognizing that we have fallen, so we can pick our self up and create something different! It's exciting to discover any pattern of resisting. This is an indication we're ready to create something kinder!

NEWS FLASH... we end up in relationships with people who treat us as we treat ourselves.

We end up with people who honor us as we honor ourselves, and then we blame them for how we're being treated. It might not be EXACTLY the same method, but the feelings we get from being in relationship with them are similar to the ones we experience in relationship to our self. Exploring this reflection and how it may be an indication of some feeling, idea, or sensation we are vibrating internally - is not wimpy stuff. It takes courage and willingness to even consider the possibility that what is in front of us is also coming from within us. Responsibility or blame? This is the important question. And hey, if you are in an abusive relationship, don't justify staying in it because of what you are reading here. Convincing yourself you can change the abuser by owning the way you abuse yourself could be more self-sabotage. We don't change other people, we attract them. Be kind to yourself! Clear out your pattern and see who shows up.

Welcome to Door #12

Cleaning the Mirror

•Take your most intimate relationship and list actions from this person you resist.

•Explore each action and list the associated feeling(s), extrapolate where you might be treating yourself in a similar manner.

•Apply Catch & Release to ideas, feelings, and sensations you consider disrespectful or unkind.

Example

David decided to apply this to his wife and listed, being ignored, she's unaffectionate, way too busy, and never has time for the activities I would like to engage in.

David recognized even as he wrote that he was the one that was always too busy to do what he enjoyed, and that he was guilty of not paying any attention to his own needs. He admitted that he constantly ignored commitments he had regarding his body, like eating well and drinking more water, but mostly his sporadic exercise routine. He ignored the fact that he sat behind his desk all day even when his body screamed or ached. He then realized he also ignored all the good things about himself, just as he accused his wife of doing. He contemplated how he never acknowledges how hard he works, how determined he is to succeed, and how committed he is to taking care of his family. He began to feel the fact that all his energy went to what needed doing and that he rarely allowed a feeling of accomplishment! It was painfully obvious that he was accusing his wife for relating to him the exact way he had been relating to himself. He understood clearly that his accusations of her were a reflection of how he was treating himself. He felt an apology coming.

David decided to apply Catch & Release to not honoring himself in life. It was an important choice. He could see how the dishonor he thought was coming from his wife had everything to do with what was going on inside of him, he was determined to own this pattern so things could change. He was the dishonoring one, he could feel it now. This awareness had him curious, he made a note to explore some other people he had been blaming and resisting. He began his release process, contemplated and felt this idea of not honoring himself. He took the time needed to deeply feel, own, and allow it all to exist. When he was ready, he let it go by stating, "Releasing the habit of not honoring myself."

He picked self respect and honor for his feeling of choice. He let himself feel his accomplishments, reviewing his life, his goodness, his determination, and perseverance.

He realized his motivation was strong and unbending, he cared deeply for his wife and children. He wanted them to have everything they needed and wanted. He let himself soak in the idea that he is not a bad guy at all. He admitted he's stubborn like a bull when it comes to succeeding, and that it is admirable how he never gives up, even when the going gets tough. His heart stirred with the value of his life and his commitment to those he loved. He let it in.

He realized he hadn't taken a day off in far too long and looked around his office with appreciation, acknowledging what he had spent his life creating successfully. Giving positive attention to himself inspired him, he felt happy and wanted to share this good feeling with his family. He phoned his wife to tell her he would be home early and would like to take everyone out to dinner. He explained his discovery to her and she expressed tremendous gratitude for him. He let it in and felt deeply satisfied.

You

MATTER

Look in the mirror and smile at the being, feel the awareness behind your eyes. It is there you will find what you have been looking for.

You matter dear companion and you always will...

CHAPTER THIRTEEN

Intuition

Getting lost in how something should appear steals the creative energy and ability to deal with how something does appear. Intuition becomes available when we are calm and present, without resistance to what is. Allow rather than resist and intuition will kick in. Allowing is being open, expanded, aware, and willing. Resisting is contracted, closed, protecting, and defending. Our most satisfying decisions are made from intuition, most likely because our intentions automatically include what is best for everyone involved. When reality is viewed from this higher-self intuitive perspective there is no hurry and there is no need to persuade. From here we trust and we always know where to step next. Right action is natural.

꩜

With awareness there comes choice. And so you are able to say: "I allow this moment to be as it is." And then, suddenly, where before there was irritation, there is now a sense of aliveness and peace. And out of that comes right action.

Eckhart Tolle

꩜

Have you ever been in a situation that required your immediate action; a car wreck, someone wounded, a child hurt, a person fell near you? As you recall how you felt, were you reaching to help automatically? If it was a situation you took charge of, do you remember how you knew what to do without even thinking? You probably moved quickly toward what instantly needed to occur without much thought. If so, you did this instinctively, intuitively. More than likely you were very present. Intuition guides us quickly in times of crisis. We never question it. It is fast pure knowing.

How do you know when you are being intuitive? Can you hear that inner voice that sometimes whispers and sometimes roars? Maybe you feel things viscerally or you get a bad taste in your mouth and somehow you just know you better pay close attention to what's going on. Intuition speaks to everyone differently and the more we listen to it the louder and clearer it becomes. The more we ignore it, the quieter it whispers.

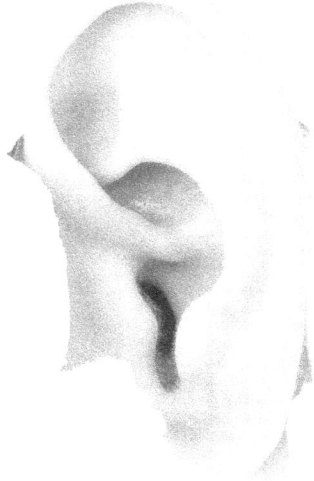

Definitions to Consider

Intuition

1. Direct perception of truth, fact, etc., independent of any reasoning process; immediate apprehension.

2. A fact, truth, etc., perceived in this way.

3. A keen and quick insight.

4. The quality or ability of having such direct perception or quick insight.

5. Philosophy **a.** an immediate cognition of an object not inferred or determined by a previous cognition of the same object. **b.** any object or truth so discerned. **c.** pure, untaught, noninferential knowledge.

Merriam-Webster's Collegiate® Dictionary Tenth Edition 1993

Intuition can be accessed deliberately in everyday situations and developed into our greatest source of comfort and trust. As our path through life is cleared of patterns geared toward avoiding feeling, we begin to appreciate the indicators feelings become. We become adept at discerning between types of feelings. We get to know our automatic reactions from our thoughtful, purposeful ones. We begin to know the difference between acting from selfish ambition and acting on behalf of all concerned. We learn to feel our quiet knowing over our loud intention to persuade. We become familiar with the nudge of intuition over the push of an ego hungry for attention or approval.

Trusting intuition is a process, an adventure with new vistas to insightful knowledge. Our intuition evolves right alongside our ability to trust our inner feelings. Trusting our inner guidance becomes a tremendous asset. We know, we trust, and we persevere, in spite of opposition or lack of conformity from outside. Intuition becomes significantly more accessible with continued application of Catch & Release to fears and doubts.

To access intuition I consider my question and then reach outward with my feeling. I become very still and extend my awareness upward, if that makes sense. I reach out in an effort to tap into the matrix I saw surrounding everyone's form when I was out of my body. During that time I witnessed a vast pool of evergy connecting everything. I sensed it had always been there, available for the asking. I felt intuitively that this field held the wisdom of all the lifetimes that had ever been lived. The energy appeared like a funnel cloud much larger than the tiny pinpoint of the form it seemed to flow into. Some people had huge funnels streaming into them and some didn't have very much at all. Everyone's human form was without question connected to the vast sea of grace. I think of this as our higher self, our intuitive self, divine intelligence, and I believe it is there waiting for us to know it and allow it. Perhaps the degree we allow it is the only degree it can respond!

Regardless of what you call this energy or how you have come to know the feeling of your own intuition the value is in recognizing it is available for you. Explore, discover, investigate and you will become very good at discerning between the folly of mind chatter and the comfort of intuition. Remove any blocks or limiting ideas you have and see what happens. What do you have to lose besides a few opinions? This is a lovely skill to help anyone you care about develop. When someone can trust their intuition they will have a fulfilling life. They become who they're meant to be, which also means they live in service to the world. Authenticity inspires a person toward their greatest self.

If we trust another's intuitive nudges over our own, we often end up traveling someone else's path through life and miss the perfection of being ourselves. Be U To Full (corny... but true).

~~

The only real valuable thing is intuition

Albert Einstein

~~

Example

To move forward from intuition I consider the question I am in a quandary about. I simply ask and then quietly wait for knowing to come. An understanding of what is next for me usually appears quickly and if I try to dissect my understanding I end up over evaluating and doubting rather than trusting.

When I am successful at maintaining a quiet mind, I understand with my feeling more than my mind. I believe this is our most powerful perch for living a fulfilling life. It is without question the most fun. When I move forward from intuition (pure feeling) I am doubt free for my next step. I feel comfortable with my plan of action, even if there is no mental or physical evidence to support my choice.

I haven't experienced voices of instruction, blinking red lights or clouds parting, although some do. There's no wrong way to do this. Trust yourself. Ask and see what happens.

Whether I am engaged in a conversation, writing, or doing dishes, I intend to be connected to this stream of Divine Intelligence. Why not? I am not afraid to ask for that big funnel cloud of love to accompany me through life. It is a slice of heaven if you ask me.

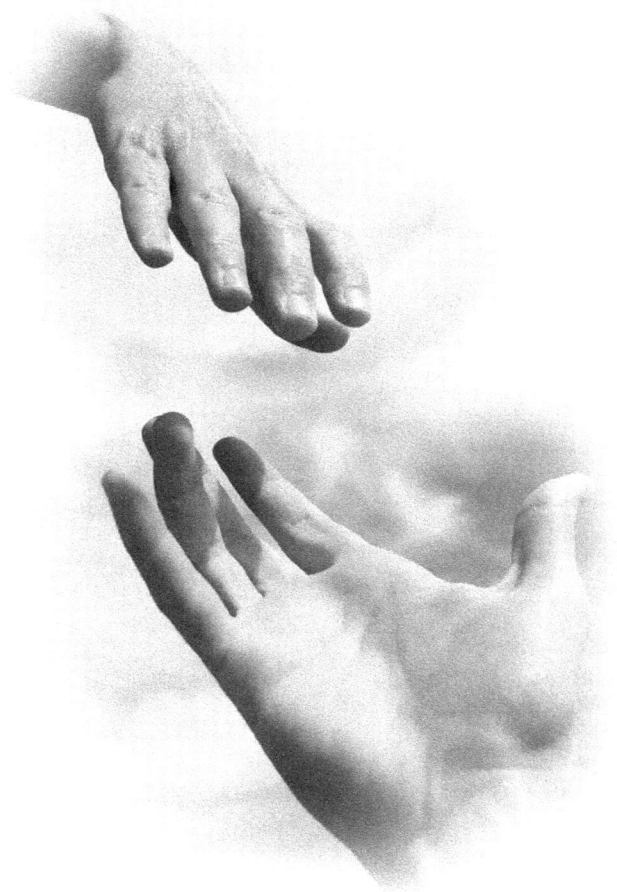

let life love you

Begin to feel the magic all around,

Talk to the wind, the blue sky,

the dancing trees,

or the pouring rain.

Ask that which you know is there

But cannot see

For assistance in knowing

Who you truly are

and what you are capable of...

And you shall have it!

CHAPTER FOURTEEN

Helping One Another

Some painful events, relationships, and ideas are so etched into our minds that we have trouble letting them go or even understanding them. There are people that get so used to carrying these old nightmares around that the painful past becomes who they are in the present. Some give up on recovering so completely that they settle into the notion of suffering forever, repeatedly, faithfully, until death do we part.

This is understandable in times of great sorrow and the kindest thing we could ever do is help our friends to take a look directly into the eyes of the pain they are sitting in and adamantly resisting. Little pieces at a time, guide them to feel and release the despair and eventually the anger so they can see there is indeed light at the end of the tunnel. Teach them to breathe deep, be willing to feel, and to reach out for help when they need a reminder that they are never alone.

If someone is excessively emotional for a long period of time, unending tears, constant sorrow, or forever angry, consider this and see if it fits (use your intuition), are they actually using emotion to resist feeling something they fear and are fixated on? I know this sounds strange and this will only make sense to a few, but it does apply to some. Being highly or uncontrollably emotional can be a way of avoiding an honest and thoughtful investigation of how they really feel about something. It can be a distraction used to resist a deeper sense of what is wrong.

There's a light
at the end of the tunnel...

...and it's not a train.

Expression borrowed with permission from Quantumusing. Inspirational and humorous greeting cards beyond the norm, enhanced with original artwork and photography visit www.Qmusing.com

Please note, there are situations where sensations of crying or being highly emotional bring great relief to someone. I am not referring to this. I am referring to someone who has been dealing with excessive anger, upset or sorrow for a long while and making no progress toward freedom. This is someone avoiding owning their feelings.

I have seen extreme anger and crying used as a form of resistance to facing a variety of ideas and life situations. In a recent conversation with a dear friend who lost her beloved a few months earlier, she explained how her excessive emotion and overwhelm was non-stop, understandably so. She wanted to let it go but didn't know how. After much listening and a strong flow of compassion I gently asked her what she was most afraid of regarding him being gone. I asked her what she did not want to experience. She surprised herself and answered quickly, "Being utterly and completely abandoned." The non-stop emotion was a method of avoiding anger and guilt deep inside. The emotion was easier than admitting and feeling her anger toward him for dying and abandoning her. We applied Catch & Release to her anger and subsequently to her immense fear of being alone and finally to her guilt over feeling this way. Her release of all this resistance was pivotal for her to begin allowing. She breathed in acceptance as her feeling of choice. She felt relaxed and present for the first time since his death. Her heart had a few moments of peace. She realized she could repeat the process and work toward feeling all the emotions that accompany healing a broken heart. She felt hope. The relief touched us both deeply.

Miracles arise out of letting go of your fear.

Out of releasing all the blocks

Which are really just the fear in disguise.

Brent Haskell, Ph.D., D.O
Journey Beyond Words
A Companion to A Course In Miracles

Being uncontrollably emotional is not bad or wrong, just recognize this may be resistance. More than likely they have no idea they are doing it. This isn't an awareness to throw in anyone's face and use to make them wrong. It is for you to know and feel so you can gently guide them by asking if there is some idea they are not wanting to feel under all the tears or anger. If they are ready, they will move their attention right to the avoided idea and begin to sense what is going on. You will know when they find the idea they are resisting and when to invite them to look it in the eye for a second or two. Your intuition will guide you. There may be many feelings in there once you get started, be patient and present.

When someone is up for this type of exploration, you will feel it. If they haven't gotten to the point where they can experience the underlying pain, so be it. They are still in the resistance stage. Help them release the resistance. If you have been practicing Catch & Release, you'll sense what to do by virtue of your personal experience of the freedom that comes with ownership. Invite them to willingly and deliberately feel their resistance... to life, to what is, to the feeling they are having, to the incident, to whatever they are resisting. Invite them to willingly feel how they push against what happened, how they deny it, avoid it, and despise it until they realize these feelings of resistance are a decision and not who they are. Have them recognize the actions of resistance as "Not I's" so they can become aware of the thinker of the thoughts and how they have a choice. Teach them how resisting their pain and sorrow makes it bigger, more real, and glues them to it. Show them they can let go of the resistance and it will help relieve some of their pain, but only if they want to. Let them know it takes feeling, owning, and deciding. Show them the steps of Catch & Release and ask them if they would like to apply it. Letting them decide is key.

It is very powerful for a person to realize that excessive emotion can actually be their way of avoiding the reality of an event, loss, or tragedy. Becoming more honest and aware is the beginning of recovery. It may take a few applications and your intuitive guidance along with great patience. Your presence and your invitation, with no attachment to how they answer, is a gift beyond measure. Whatever feeling they are ready to release will always open the door to the next layer. Each release of resistance will allow more acceptance and peace. Trust the process of unraveling. People typically reach for more once they realize the freedom that accompanies ownership. If they don't and they've got their heels dug in, there is only one thing you can do. Apply Catch & Release to any resistance you have to their suffering. Release your inner worry or fear so you can allow their feelings to exist without being afraid. Be present with them in a surrendered state of allowing and it invites them to open their heart and experience what is there. Your vibration of care is how doors open and paths to healing are revealed. Believe in them and show them the way by example! This is true friendship.

If this person is you, please be so kind to yourself as you proceed toward owning where you find yourself. If you feel ready to look your trauma in the eye and begin, please invite a friend to read this chapter and sit with you as you take your steps toward ownership. Apply Catch & Release tenderly. Be as gentle and loving toward yourself in this process as you would a dear friend experiencing the same heartbreak.

When we resist emotional pain it hurts worse.

When we resist emotional pain it becomes larger.

When we resist pain of any kind it becomes more consuming.

When we stay numb to avoid pain it waits, lingering and ever present.

When we resist physical pain it becomes increasingly intolerable.

When we resist something inside we often attract it from the outside.

When we resist anything for too long it becomes an appendage.

When we allow and take steps toward ownership we eventually reach peace with what is. This leads to a fresh kind of honesty that allows us to create a new reality to experience, more in alignment with the conscious decisions we are choosing to make.

⤳⤳

Nothing can bring you peace but yourself.

Ralph Waldo Emerson

⤳⤳

Welcome to Door #14

Allowing Help

As a team apply Catch & Release to a painful event either of you feel ready to unravel.

•List any unresolved event you felt excessive and uncontrollable emotion over with no peaceful solution.

•With a friend explore the situation by asking what idea(s), sensation(s), or feeling(s) you are avoiding experiencing and apply Catch & Release.

Note: This may require repeating until the process feels complete to both parties. Be spacious and allowing of the unfolding.

Example

David knew immediately upon reading this chapter what he needed to let go of. He felt brutally betrayed by his ex-wife and never let go of his anger and resentment toward her. He had never wanted to. He boiled inside with the thought of her and how she manipulated to destroy his life. He wasn't very comfortable asking his current wife to help him with this issue. But after some thought, he realized she was the perfect person. She had been asking David for years to let this upset go, explaining how it was hurting everyone, especially the kids.

David had already been talking to her about the Catch & Release process and sharing his successes. When he told her his intentions she eagerly volunteered to be the one to invite him toward taking responsibility and ownership of the feelings he was carrying around. She reviewed the steps in chapter four, Catch & Release, and was excited to help him finally reach some peace with this whole thing.

They sat together on the couch. David was very uncomfortable. She invited him to relax and tenderly invited him to take a couple of deep breaths. He was glad she was there. She very intuitively invited him to explain what he was so upset about to get him to move in the direction they needed to go so they could find the underlying feeling he had been avoiding with all his emotion.

David began, "She took my life savings, my children, my house, and never looked back. Most of all she betrayed me by trying to turn my children against me. She told them I was no longer a man of faith and that I was not a good father for them. All because I didn't conform to her beliefs or the doctrines of her Church and instead found my own path of faith. She is so stuck on her religious beliefs that she tried to have the kids avoid me and feel sorry for me as though I was the Antichrist himself. Since she was given custody she brainwashed all of them into believing her and siding with her for so long that I missed many years with them. John still doesn't trust me (his youngest child). To this day he keeps his distance, believing I am the one that hurt his mother. She remarried immediately and tried to get the kids to call her new husband 'dad,' claiming he was more of a father than I. I was infuriated, helpless, and hated the thoughts that controlled my mind. I hate what she did to me and my relationships with my children. I believe she was all set to have her new husband before we ever split up. I think she had all her ducks in a row. They lived off of my hard work, he freeloaded in my house, with my kids, on my money. She deserves to suffer."

David was red faced and spewing. He was shaking with emotion. His wife gently said, "You may be right about everything. She may be a very bad person, but what is most important is for you to let go of the emotions and feelings you keep choosing to carry through time. So David, What is the idea you are resisting feeling about all of this, what do you NOT want to experience regarding all of this?"

He became emotional in a different way the moment he knew his answer. "I don't want her to get away with this crime and injustice. She should pay for the suffering she's caused." He hated that this idea just came out of his mouth but he felt it deep inside, "How can someone be so cruel anyway. I am a good person and just because I don't agree with her ideas about God, Jesus, or how to raise children, she shouldn't punish me and take my kids away. Isn't that the opposite of what Jesus taught anyway? Doesn't the bible invite us to practice unconditional love and patience enough to let a person find their way towards truth? She totally discounted all the good in me." He put his head down in his hands and sighed deeply, beginning to see that he was doing to her exactly what he was accusing her of doing to him. His wife waited while David let the waves of feeling move through him and then she softly asked, "So what is the idea you don't want to feel?" Without lifting his head he whispered barely audible, "That I hurt my children, that it is my fault. I told the truth about my faith and couldn't pretend to want the same thing she wanted for our kids and I ended up hurting everyone. I don't want to feel the idea that I am the one who harmed my relationships with my children."

Being very wise, his wife invited him to first feel the resistance to this idea and release it before he ventured into feeling the actual idea of hurting his kids. She knew he needed to let go of his resistance to the concept first or he would not be able to experience or feel the idea at all. Resisting the idea would block his ability to feel it and let it go. She said, "David, feel your resistance to being the one that harmed your kids. Just feel how much you hate this idea. Breathe it in and let it be there for a minute." David took a few deep breaths and let the emotion be there. She stayed quiet until he said, "Okay, I feel it. I feel how I have been resisting this idea for the last ten years. I get it. I am the one who keeps pushing against this idea and the feelings that go with it. I am the one keeping it all alive with my resistance to it." She invited again, "Now just feel your resistance to the idea, own the resistance as yours, and see how resisting has been your decision.

Acknowledge it as something you gave birth to and when you are ready, breathe it out. Let it go, visualize it leaving your body, your mind, your spirit. Let go of the resistance." He followed her instructions and as he exhaled he stated, "Releasing this resistance." He took one more deep breath and let it all go. David lifted his head and looked into her soft eyes with gratitude. His relief was tangible.

She asked him if he was ready to finish. Lovingly he called her a drill sergeant. She explained, "You let go of the resistance to the idea, now you can let go of the crazy notion that you harmed your children by following your heart! David, you know trusting one's self is the greatest lesson a parent could ever teach their child. Look at our kids' honey, they believe in themselves! Being told what to believe robs a child of finding their own path." He was enjoying her little rampage. She persisted, "Now look this ridiculous notion right in the eye and feel it as an idea you've mistakenly focused on." David obeyed and explored the guilt, grief and heartache associated with this concept. It took a while to allow the sensations. Finally, he understood it was all a "Not I." Deeply appreciating his new awareness, he was ready. He declared, "Releasing the idea that I harmed my kids by following my heart!"

He looked up and his wife had tears in her eyes. They both felt a tremendous release. They shared an intuitive knowing that something wonderful could now happen for the whole family. Forgiveness could finally begin to heal the broken hearts and love would lead the way.

love

Love is patient and kind

Love does not envy or boast

It is not arrogant or rude.

It does not insist on its own way

It is not irritable or resentful

It does not rejoice at wrongdoing, but rejoices with the truth.

Love bears all things, believes all things, hopes all things, endures all things.

Love never ends.

1 Corinthians 13:4–8a ESV

CHAPTER FIFTEEN

Forgive Forgive Forgive

Our single most self destructive act is non-forgiveness. Our enormous MIS-TAKE is believing we are somehow punishing our abuser by keeping our hatred, blame, or resentment in place. The exact opposite is true. We are hurting ourselves, our body, and our potential by carrying this resentment forward through time. The vibration of blame we cling to draws more of itself toward us. Meaning we end up seeing, feeling, and attracting similar scenarios of victimhood and betrayal until we are able to forgive and release the negative energy. Again, the incidents may not be the exact same in detail, but our deep sense of being treated unfairly prevails through life.

Thoughts, intentions, and words are alive. They take up space, carry weight, and vibrate with their content. As I moved away from my dying body in the hospital I visually experienced this phenomenon. My body was filled with non-forgiveness and it had clearly crippled me in every way imaginable, emotionally, physically, and spiritually. What we think matters. How we feel emotionally has everything to do with our physical health and vitality. The willingness to release painful memories, resentments, and events transforms lives.

෴

Not forgiving someone is like taking poison and waiting for someone else to die.

Dr. Christiane Northrup

World renowned scientist, Gregg Braden has spent a lifetime enacting thoroughly documented studies which prove that sound and feeling emit a vibration that affect our body, the environment, and the world. During Gregg Braden's program entitled Healing Hearts/Healing Nations: The Science of Peace and the Power of Prayer, he explains one of these experiments in depth and portrays how we are energetic magnets.

Gregg Braden explains:

"What was discovered was that the DNA changed its shape according to the feelings of the researchers: 1. When the researchers felt gratitude, love and appreciation, the DNA responded by relaxing and the strands unwound. The length of the DNA became longer. 2. When the researchers felt anger, fear, frustration, or stress, the DNA responded by tightening up. It became shorter and switched off many of our DNA codes! If you've ever felt 'shutdown' by negative emotions, now you know why, your body was equally shutdown too.

The shutdown of the DNA codes was reversed when feelings of love, joy, gratitude and appreciation were felt by the researchers. This experiment was later followed up by testing HIV positive patients. They discovered that feelings of love, gratitude and appreciation created 300,000 times more strength to the disease than they had without those feelings. So here's the answer to what can help you stay well, stay in feelings of joy, love, gratitude and appreciation! This illustrates a new recognized form of energy that connects all of creation. This energy appears to be a tightly woven web that connects all matter. Essentially we're able to influence this web of creation through our vibration. This is how we create our reality - by choosing it with our feelings. Our feelings are activating the timeline via the web of creation, which connects all of the energy and matter of the Universe. Remember that the law of the Universe is that we attract what we focus on. If you are focused on fearing whatever may come, you are sending a strong message to the Universe to send you whatever you fear. **"**

It seems we often confuse forgiving someone with having to trust them again. Forgiving does not mean we have to crawl into bed with our abuser or go out to dinner with them. It means we set ourselves free from constant judgment and have faith in the mechanics of consciousness to do what it always does, remind everyone who they are being. This is not our job, punishment is not our job, and our effort to hurt someone in return only exacerbates the problem. Throughout history we have tried to punish and control abusers with very little success. They resist being dominated and spew anger and hatred into the world even more, whenever given the chance. Paying punishment forward is not the answer. As we intuitively understand how reality reflects our inner state, we compassionately recognize that there is a current guiding all of humanity to discover who they are being. The vibration they emit will always bring them a life that mirrors how they treat others. It is the way of energy. It is the law of attraction.

Perhaps we have forgiveness confused…

Believing that forgiving an abuser means we're weak.

Believing that if we forgive another, the mistake will occur again.

Believing if we forgive them, they win.

Believing that forgiving lets them off the hook, never realizing the hook of not forgiving is in us.

Resisting an abuser attaches us to them. Resistance adds attention and energy to the incident or upset. Resisting grows the very reality we are pushing against into more pain and suffering. Forgiving, on the other hand, frees up our creative energy so it can be directed toward dreams.

If we are hurting and unable to successfully apply Catch & Release to a repeating pattern, chances are we have someone to forgive. Yes, this person could be us.

≈≈

As you think, you vibrate. And it is your vibrational offering that equals your point of attraction. So what you are thinking and what is coming back to you is always a vibrational match.

Abraham-Hicks, The Law of Attraction

≈≈

If you are caught in a loop of self punishment, sabotaging your success repeatedly, not crossing finish lines, and giving up on yourself, this chapter is going to be your favorite! Not forgiving yourself is The GRAND MASTER of self-sabotage. This energy of self abnegation (whether conscious or not) vibrates outwardly instructing a world of people to copy and conform. Failure to forgive yourself becomes a magnet to types of people that will prove your feelings of unworthiness. This non-forgiveness of self vibration invites financial endeavors of the same caliber and for some, ill health. The body breaks down from any habit of pretending, ignoring, and denying ownership for cruel and damaging actions (toward self or another) that we are unwilling to admit or own. Our secrets eat us alive. Some have gotten so good at pretending they didn't commit any errors that they can't see what is right in front of them. Until they look, become honest, and turn their ability to feel and experience back on. Freedom from repeating patterns goes hand in hand with ownership.

We are harder on ourselves than anyone else ever could be. Not forgiving ourselves can equal unconsciously making decisions to insure we fail or suffer. Some sabotage their own healing, some make sure they block any chance for abundance, while others stay in hurtful relationships or habits… all to pay for mistakes they have been unable to address or forgive.

Forgiveness becomes more viable with the realization that your thoughts in present time are causing you the pain, not the incident that happened long ago or even yesterday. Non-forgiveness could include any act we feel guilty for, from stealing a dollar out of someone's wallet, abandoning a friend or child, all the way to a car accident that ended tragically. It is the perpetual belief in our guilt and the turmoil inside of us that destroys lives throughout time, not the incident that happened long ago. We can feel the pain of an event, release it, and make profound restitution as a gift to the world. The trick is to stop giving the event life by telling it. Let the story end... allow healing to occur. We can forgive.

15

Welcome to Door #15

Decide to Forgive

•List any action or experience you have been unwilling or unable to forgive another for.

•Discover and list the feeling(s), Idea(s), and sensation(s) you have NOT wanted to feel regarding each action. Apply Catch & Release to each feeling. Complete by cultivating and filling up with a sensation of choice.

•Explore for an interaction or circumstance where you may have hurt another in any way similar to the way you felt hurt. If so, own it by saying and feeling, "I have done that before." Let your intuition guide you toward any action you feel important to correct the mistake.

•Repeat step 1 and 2 on any action you have been unwilling or unable to forgive yourself for. Be sure to choose a feeling of choice when you are complete with the release and soak in the sensation.

Example

Sally listed - Her friend for giving up and not fighting harder to live (Sally lost her best and dearest friend to cancer) and her mother for letting her father abuse her. Sally was more eager to begin the work on forgiving herself.

Sally chose to work on her mother. She asked herself what she didn't want to feel and became a bit overwhelmed by the stream of thoughts that flooded her mind… being used, being unimportant, my mother not caring about me, being punished by God, being a mistake (they didn't want children), and then the idea came, my mom thought it was all my fault, that I deserved to be abused. Sally had a feeling this was what she had never forgiven her mother for. She had worked with many of the other ideas on self help courses but the dreaded feeling of being a bad person, never went away. She blamed her mother, often, for the fact that she had to live her life with this feeling of never being good enough or never doing enough. If anything bad happened around her Sally automatically felt it was her fault, regardless of whether it was or not. She was angry and steeped in resentment toward her mother, believing the condition of her life was more her mother's fault than her own.

Sally made a list of her feelings toward her mother; uncaring, selfish, wants everything her way, disconnected, irresponsible, horrible mother, blames others for everything, victim of life, expects others to take care of her. The list triggered a lot of old feelings. She had to stand up and walk around for a minute to get some energy moving. She was ready. She really did want to forgive her mother and let this pattern of resentment go.

She inhaled nice and slow and began relaxing, quieting, allowing, owning and accepting. She felt herself being used by her mother. After a few moments, she noticed that the feeling wasn't so terrible. She surrendered and felt what it was like being unimportant, ignored, and wrong. She willingly experienced feeling like a victim of life. Sally felt more aware with each release. When she was ready to own and allow the last idea she looked down at the words… 'my mother thought it was all my fault and believed she couldn't change how things were,' Sally had a weird feeling deep in her gut. It was an intuitive signal. She kept looking at the words and rolling them around until she had an insight, "I have that same feeling about life, like it's not my fault how I feel and it's not my fault how things work out."

Something strange started happening inside her, she felt like someone had pulled a rug out from under her and everything was trying to find a new place to settle. Slowly she considered how she didn't take responsibility very well for her own life, her own body, her own circumstances, much like she was accusing her mother of doing. She thought about her own daughter and began to see how she was repeating the pattern. She was very sad. She began to apply Catch & Release to the blame and non-forgiveness she held onto for her mother for being this way. She sat quietly for a while, owning the ideas and feelings as hers. When she was ready she released the feeling by deciding, "Releasing blame towards my mother." She repeated it again and felt the feeling of blame and non-forgiveness flow out of her body. She was very still inside sensing a different her.

Sally was reviewing what had just happened and she felt great compassion for her mom. She had been angry with her for so long, holding a grudge most of her life. Until now, she hadn't realized she was duplicating her mother's behavior. She clearly understood, "I've done that before," and added, "I am doing it right now." She was seeing so many similarities. She realized she needed to apply this process to herself and forgive herself for many mistakes.

Sally completed the last step of Catch & Release selecting the sensation of, 'taking responsibility for how she feels in life.' She contemplated what that would look like, with her daughter, her husband, her body, and really explored how this would change her experience of being Sally. She was gentle with herself as she realized how little she had done this in life. She allowed the idea and sensation in as much as possible, imagining the feeling of being fully responsible flowing through her cells, her mind, her heart, and into her world. She knew this would become a stronger sensation once she forgave herself.

Sally had clarity on the second part of the exercise. Undoubtedly she was behaving very much like what she saw and blamed her mother for being. She whispered out loud one more time, "I've done that too, mom. I've done that too."

Sally decided to wait for a while to begin the self forgiveness process. She knew there was much to address, mostly for how she had treated her own daughter and not been there for her. She wanted to allow this new understanding to soak in a bit before she continued. She also wanted to call her mother and apologize. She was beginning to understand, at an entirely new level, how all her attention had been going to what was wrong with her mother, with life, and with herself and how it was her energy going in that direction that made it all so consuming and real. She was determined to move her focus to the goodness in her mother and flow it toward what she wanted to feel instead of to her old stories. She was determined to become strong at pointing her attention toward dreams.

Forgiveness Success Story

A dear friend elected to apply Catch & Release to her anger toward her ex-husband, and it just wouldn't go away – an indication there is something to forgive.

She was very frustrated. I invited her to specify what he did to her and what she was most angry about.

She explained, "I have been divorced for 25 years and I just can't let go of what that man did to me. He abandoned me and my daughter. I have tried everything I know and Catch & Release won't work, not completely, it always comes back. I want to stop carrying this baggage around."

She was angry as she spoke and I invited her to explore if there were any circumstances in her life where she had acted in the same or a similar manner as her ex-husband. She was open and willing. It took less than a minute of

introspection. She looked up, wide eyed and white as a sheet. "Yes, oh my gosh yes. I have done the very same thing. I have done that before to someone else."

She became very sad with the insight, she felt the pain she had caused another and was very sorry. She considered what she could do to apologize and make up for it.

I invited her to feel that her ex-husband and she weren't so different and that mistakes can be turned into good.

She spoke softly, very present as she shared, "My feelings of anger toward him melted." Shocked she whispered "It happened instantaneously with seeing this inside of me."

⌒⌒

Many have found it very powerful to look and see if what they were blaming another for was an action they had committed themselves. To some degree or in some way it always was. They found the phrase *"I've done that before,"* provided an opportunity for ownership and release. The phrase became very useful in the moment they caught themselves pointing their finger outward.

One person reported that this phrase transformed his attitude on the freeway, another used it very successfully with her employees and a neighbor of mine used it at home often, inviting the whole family to join her in letting go of blame.

Next time you're getting angry, upset or frustrated toward someone consider: *"Have you done that before!"*

⮑⮐

Two Wolves

A Native American grandfather was talking to his grandson about how he felt about the tragedy. He said, "I feel as if I have two wolves fighting in my heart. One wolf is the vengeful, angry, violent one. The other wolf is the loving, compassionate one."

The grandson asked him, "Which wolf will win the fight in your heart?"

The grandfather answered, "The one I feed."

Native American Story

⮑⮐

CHAPTER SIXTEEN

The Desire Diet

Our body is the collection point of our thoughts, our ideas, and our emotions. This vehicle we are riding in through life is the action spot of our universe. It is where thought meets intention, where rubber meets the road, and dreams become realities! Our relationship with our body is the most telling relationship of all. We are walking around in the greatest teacher in our world. Our body is our point of manifestation.

Do you listen to your body? Do you honor your body? Do you like your body? Do you care about your body? Are you friends with your body? Do you have a lot of body, a little body, a fast body, a slow body, are you somebody or are you nobody? (Sounds like Dr. Seuss).

What do you want regarding your body? Do you put attention and energy toward your physical goals? Toward being healthy? Or, do you put more attention and energy toward resisting pain and physical nightmares? You are powerful, and where you point your attention and energy matters! Resistance makes things grow, Catch & Release lets them go.

Here is a miracle diet. We call it the desire diet!

Feel this; if you resist eating, you will have attention on food 24/7. Resistance makes things bigger, more real! You will notice skinny people EVERYWHERE! You may even resent any-body walking around in a size 10 or less. You may secretly feel jealous of people who eat whatever they want to. Unaware that your resistance to high calorie food has become a magnet to your focus on anything to do with high calorie foods. Any resistance to cake, carbs, or that shot of Baileys, glues your attention and energy to those things. For example, if you resist sweet foods more than others, those will be the ones you sneak. Our opposition fuels whatever we are opposing. Chances are you want everything you are not supposed to have even more so when you diet.

Diets are based on someone's ability to resist. This is ironic and backwards and makes things much more difficult than they need to be. Resisting eating certain foods always adds discouragement and despair into our eating experience. Some may even feel like a victim of their body condition, compounding the discouragement. This is due to the resistance to feeling something.

We may lose weight by following a strict diet providing we have a huge amount of willpower and can force ourselves to go against our unhealthy cravings. This can work for a while, however, there's an easier way. A kinder way!

This solution is working well for people. Here's the trick. Every time you feel yourself moving into an action of resistance to food, to your body, or to your health... stop and notice the sensation inside. Apply Catch & Release on the spot. You can do this quickly and efficiently now. Just look the feeling of resistance in the eye, breathe it in, and decide with all your heart to breathe it out! Here's the best part... instantly visualize the body you want. Imagine manifesting that body, walking in that body, dancing in that body, and loving in that body. Put your attention immediately toward the feeling you long to have living in your dream body! Imagine this healthy happy you. Flow your attention into your goal, your desire, your wishes, your hopes, and your passion to feel amazing. FEED DESIRE and watch it grow.

So... a perfect, healthy, strong, good looking body walks by and you feel envious, irritated, or even hungry. Stop! Condemning someone else's manifestation of what you would like for yourself is an indicator! Release this resistance so you can celebrate the success of others (genuinely celebrating another's success is always a short-cut to your own goal). Notice what you feel. Own it as your thought, your idea, and your sensation. This is a fabulous and very worthwhile Catch. Remember, you gave birth to the thought you can certainly give it death. Look the feeling you discovered right in the eye. Be present with it and feel it. Breathe it out! Experience one feeling at a time. Don't try to do several and sabotage yourself. For example, if you feel frustration breathe in and allow the discomfort of this one sensation, let it be there, then release it by saying, "Releasing frustration." Call the feeling by name and say the words with intention. Your decision to release the reaction is a pivotal part of the process.

Resistance has many faces when it comes to consumption, being unhealthy, and pain. Be willing to feel whatever shows up; resentment, stubbornness, blame, sadness, anger, victimhood, etc. Becoming aware of the feeling inside when you reach to eat or drink something you have previously decided is not good for you, is very revealing. What we discover rarely has to do with food. When we learn to recognize and own the aspect of our SELF that ACTS AGAINST our SELF, and release it, life transforms. Any habits of self sabotage regarding food are usually affecting our ability to create abundance, fulfilling relationships, and forgiveness. Committing to this practice of Catching & Releasing what shows up the moment you are going to give up on yourself–will open doors to dreams. This is where the rubber meets the road!

If you are out in public and don't have time to be thorough with Catch & Release, here is a short cut. Use this for a temporary fix and be sure to set aside time to later discover the resisted feelings that came up during the incident and apply Catch & Release to each one (powerful). Now, the quick fix, the one to practice the moment you are about to give in… quickly and determinedly picture yourself in the body you are dreaming to have. See your dream body right in front of you! Move your focus over to what you want to look like, what you want to feel like. Imagine this image stealth, healthy, vibrant, and right in front of you. Feel the strength of this amazing body. Feel how energetic and happy it is. The more you visualize your dream body in front of you and feed this goal the power of your strong desire, your attention, and your hope, the more real it will become. Your attention and energy create your reality. Use it to manifest!

Every time you shift your energy out of resistance and over to what you want, something profound happens with your ability to decide and not waver. Focusing on what you want, with as much passion as you can muster, strengthens your will to do whatever it takes to have it. With each application you enhance your skill level. With every drop of attention you release from your feeling of hopelessness (or whatever resistance spells for you regarding your body) and direct over to your picture, your dream, you will be making your goal more alive and your resistance less real. Your ability to implement this action in response to food will improve with every application.

Students often place a photo of the body type they desire where they can see it throughout the day. They look at the picture, imagine having that body as theirs, and feel the strength of living in it. They add more attention to their dream with each look, with each desire. Doors open and insights occur as we reach for what we want more frequently than focusing on what we resist. We begin to grasp the mechanics of accomplishment in an unforgettable way. We feel better. Perseverance becomes fun rather than impossible.

If you can promise yourself to shift your attention toward your goal each time you catch yourself dabbling in self criticism or doubt, you will become very good friends with YOU (a lifelong endeavor for many). If you create a practice of focusing on the image you long to have, release resistance, and spend a little time each day cultivating and imagining this desired shape as yours, you will feel an increase in your determination and excitement in short order! This is the fuel for your passion! Passion creates reality!

The most transformative aspect of this undertaking will be how you decided to be responsible for what you are feeling regarding your body. You didn't need a guru, a coach, or anybody outside of you to achieve this kind behavior. You did it out of harvesting your passion and pointing it toward what you want. If you can do it once, you can do it forever. You begin to truly believe in yourself. Success begins to course through your veins!

As you develop the skill to direct more of your creative

energy into what you do want and remove it from what you don't want there is no possibility of failure. If you blow it now and then, so what, no beating yourself up! Making yourself wrong is a trick of the ego to hook you back into an old familiar pattern of discouragement and resisting. Don't fall for that inner dialogue of not being good enough. Catch & Release and start again from where you are. Visualize yourself as you dream to be, and go for it! Never stop! Never give up!

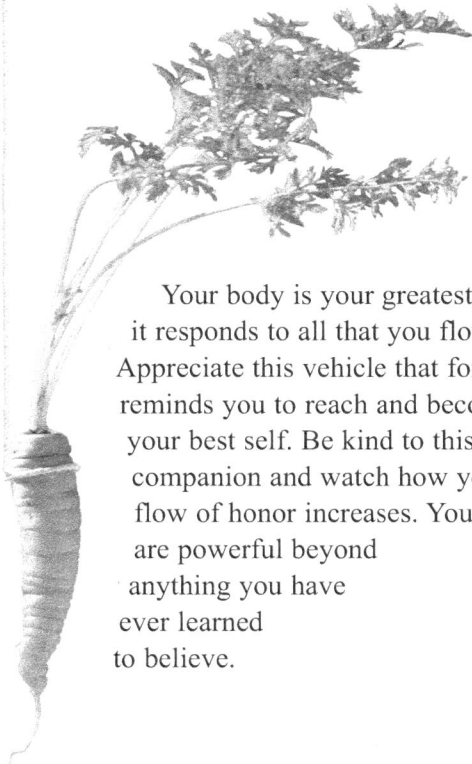

Your body is your greatest teacher as it responds to all that you flow toward it. Appreciate this vehicle that forever reminds you to reach and become your best self. Be kind to this dear companion and watch how your flow of honor increases. You are powerful beyond anything you have ever learned to believe.

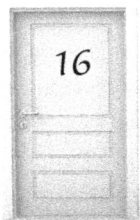

Welcome to Door #16

Your Body... *your friend*

•Recall a time when you over indulged or behaved unkind toward your body. Discover any feelings of resistance (stubbornness, orneriness, blame, anger, etc.). Apply Catch & Release to each sensation individually. After each release fill up with a feeling of choice (self-confidence, health, vitality, joy, peace, etc.).

•Imagine your body healthy, fit, and as you would like it to be. See this image in front of you, smiling at you, beckoning you to believe in yourself. Notice details and etch them into your mind.

•Practice flowing attention into your healthy happy body image, often, and forever. Put more attention into your desired body than you're flowing into a resisted body. Watch the magic.

Example

Hmmmm. It appears David and Sally have both discovered their respective white horses and are presently riding like the wind toward their new realities! Well adorned in willingness to Catch & Release any resistance they encounter and filled with passion to manifest their dreams, they are no longer available. Henceforth this concludes the example portions of the exercises as we have been unable to locate them.

No worrying, we are certain David and Sally will live happily ever after!

﹋

Passionately

Releasing resistance clears the path to passion and enthusiasm.

Excitement leads to excellence in every aspect of life!

﹋

CHAPTER SEVENTEEN

The Inner Winner

Who doesn't love winning? From an early age we've witnessed that with winning comes a prize. The reward can include admiration, loyalty, money, a trophy, a cup cake, or a simple pat on the back from someone we adore. We love winning!

Winning is one thing. Beating someone else is another. Can we engage in light competition with a game of checkers, golf, or cards without it boiling down to being better than another? Do we need someone to lose so we can feel like a winner? Or, is there another way?

∽∾

Forget your opponents; always play against par.

Sam Snead

∽∾

Definition to Consider

Competition - The act of competing, as for profit or a prize; rivalry.

Merriam-Webster's Collegiate® Dictionary Tenth Edition 1993

There are many definitions of competition. More important than how we explain its components or argue about its spoils, is what we feel and face when participating in it. Are we inspired, stressed, relaxed, happy, sleeping well, or antsy when engaged in a competitive arena. Do we feel compassionate, eager, connected to our fellow humans, and excited about our projects for the day? Can we enjoy another's win as easy as our own? Or, are we heavy hearted and annoyed with others when they out produce or outsmart us?

Many of us have automatic and unconscious motivations to win or be better than others. These motivations ultimately sabotage our intuitive peace of mind. For example; some purchase a car beyond their means to establish a mark of superiority. Some adopt pretense as a strategy to rub elbows with certain people and lose their authentic self in the game. Some push employees to close a deal even if it means breaching ethical policy or health safety. Some spend a great deal of money they don't have in the presence of another they revere. Some parents compete by flaunting their children's grades and accomplishments, using their children to feel superior. Some parents push children to achieve their own personal ideals to establish rank or gain approval from peers, unaware they are stifling the unique passion of the child.

The actions listed are not necessarily bad or wrong, it is the motivation behind them that warrants investigation. When we are stimulated by serving only ourselves, we eventually suffer. The results are never fulfilling, not for very long. The new car is nice for a while but then reality sets in and we look for something else shiny and new. We have a closet full of expensive clothes and jewelry but who are we without them? Who are we in relationship to the child we didn't listen to or encourage toward discovering their own dream? Is our connection with them honorable and filled with mutual respect? Who are we without the material possessions; do they give meaning to our lives? Do they fulfill our purpose on earth?

Material possessions come and go. It is how we feel when our head hits the pillow that matters.

Consider the viewpoint, winning or succeeding without respect and appreciation for the competition is self-sabotage in one of its ugliest performances. If how we treat others always returns to us, and if what we flow out always comes back to us, then we're sabotaging our goal to enjoy life with each effort to manipulate another for personal gain. Using another to benefit self is motivated by resistance to failure (which attracts failure). It is not an act of good intention filled with determination toward creating success (which attracts success).

Unfortunately, temptation to ignore ethics or intuitive moral code in favor of accomplishment, personal wealth, or accumulation of material objects occurs frequently. The examples abound, from the insane Texas-Cheerleader-Murdering-Mom who desperately wanted her daughter to win the cheerleading competition, to Wall Street's Bernie Madoff who destroyed countless lives with greed and corruption. To gain what? To feel how? For how long? They both lost what mattered most in the end.

What goes out always comes in.

Exploiting another for personal gain is a prescription for failure. We may end up with cars, jewelry, wine, women,

men and song, but what did it cost? We lose our self respect, end up lonely and unfulfilled, and need medication to sleep. So, what were the benefits again?

≈≈

Most people laugh when one suggests any kind of system other than the one currently in place, saying that behaviors such as competing and killing and the "victor taking the spoils" are what makes their civilization great! Most people even think there is no other natural way to be, that it is the nature of humans to behave in this manner, and that to act any other way would kill the inner spirit that drives man to succeed. (No one asks the question, "Succeed at what?")

Neale Donald Walsch

≈≈

If you want to have some real fun and create profound success, consider this... playful competition with an aligned effort to manifest a reality that benefits others and shares the wealth with all involved is brilliantly rewarding. Not to mention effective and inspiring. Cooperation is fulfilling and it reminds participants and recipients how powerful the focus of attention is when directed as an aligned team toward good for all! This will not only transform a family and any group of professionals, but also the world. When people are motivated by empowering one another toward success,

something magical transpires. With good intentions as the driving force our ability to manifest multiplies. If you truly want to enjoy success, enjoy helping others succeed.

There are numerous Cinderella stories, wins in sports, miraculous talent competitions where the underdog sings like an angel for their dying mother. These wins are so lovely to witness and feel in our hearts because the actions of the competitor are selfless. They are motivated by doing something that will benefit another. Many a competition has been championed by a team determined to gift a dying coach, or succeed to honor or benefit an injured teammate. When our efforts are ignited by sincere care and compassion for another, inspiration fills us with unusual ability. When we move forward with an open heart rather than a self serving hunger, the energy that creates worlds (the invisible) seems to join in.

If we are eager to cultivate success, health, and happiness, I propose we begin looking for how to help others achieve the same. Just for fun! As we inspire and encourage others toward their joy, there is an overflow that simultaneously contributes to our own path of success. We do not need a tragedy like 911 or Columbine or the Tsunami of 3-11, to remind us to care about our human family. Let's consider the benefit of others to be as relevant as our own for a while and notice what happens in our hearts, in our personal relationships, and with our sleep patterns.

To experience the deep truth of this phenomenon one must decide to take responsibility for what motivates them and be willing to release any habit of exploiting others for personal gain. Unimaginable success comes with waking to the knowledge that we are all in this together and when one wins, we all win! When competition is used creatively and cooperatively, it fosters greater connection within our work environments, inspires honoring relationships, and creates a better world for future generations.

Welcome to Door #17

Clear Your Path to Success

•Admit if there is someone you have secretly wanted to fail or suffer.

• List the experiences, feelings, ideas, and sensations you are resisting.

• Apply Catch & Release to all resistance.

• Explore filling up with the sensation(s) of assisting another toward success.

you • me • WE

We are all dependent on one another, every soul of us on earth.

George Bernard Shaw

Now join your hands, and with your hands your hearts.

William Shakespeare

There is the sky, which is all men's together.

Euripides

We may have all come on different ships, but we're in the same boat now.

Martin Luther King Jr.

The only thing that will redeem mankind is cooperation.

Bertrand Russell

CHAPTER EIGHTEEN

A Compassionate Heart

As you let go of pain and worry you assist world consciousness. Every drop of kindness you share moves out from you into your surroundings, like ripples in a still pond when a rock is thrown in. You add something precious to the world with your determination to become a better person. Your care contributes to the overall energy that envelopes us all. You matter.

Every thought you have is alive and comes with a feeling, an interpretation, and an experience. Taking responsibility for how you view yourself and others and owning what you think and flow into life is not a small undertaking. However, it is the work at hand. Taking full responsibility for what we experience is the only path that leads to designing a life we love to live. Every goal, every dream, and all hope for a harmonious family, a healthy body, a pleasant work environment, and a kind planet evolve from owning where we find ourselves right now.

As you become more aware and responsible for what you share and deposit into the world you will not only transform your life... but also the lives of those nearest to you. They will feel genuine possibility in your presence and appreciate how doors magically open while in your company.

~~

Each moment that you are happy is a gift to the rest of the world.

Harry Palmer

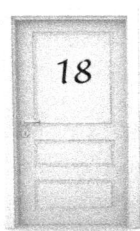

Welcome to Door #18

Choosing Compassion

⇒⇐

Love is an expression of the willingness to create space in which something is allowed to change.

Harry Palmer

⇒⇐

Instructions: This exercise can be done anywhere that people congregate (airports, malls, parks, beaches, etc.). It should be done on strangers, unobtrusively, from some distance. Try to do all five steps on the same person. Expected results are a personal sense of peace.

Step 1 With attention on the person, repeat to yourself:
Just like me, this person is seeking some happiness for his/her life.

Step 2 With attention on the person, repeat to yourself:
Just like me, this person is trying to avoid suffering in his/her life.

Step 3 With attention on the person, repeat to yourself:
Just like me, this person has known sadness, loneliness and despair.

Step 4 With attention on the person, repeat to yourself:
Just like me, this person is seeking to fulfill his/her needs.

Step 5 With attention on the person, repeat to yourself:
Just like me, this person is learning about life.

Variations:

1. May be done by couples and family members to increase understanding of each other.

2. May be done on old enemies and antagonists still present in your memories.

3. May be done on other life forms.

⇌

You are powerful beyond anything you have believed yourself to be! You are filled with everything it takes to create a life experience you treasure. The energy moving through your body and mind is akin to a beam of light, so bright it gives existence to whatever you point it toward.

This is POWER...

This is YOU!

You have a stream of energy that creates worlds moving through you. This is what you do in every moment of your day... ignite what you focus on.

As you become more aware of your creator beam, you begin to see that every person you encounter has their own. They have a stream, a potent force made of expectation, and it will always and forever manifest exactly what it's being pointed at.

When we point our light toward desires, we manifest dreams. When we remind others how to point theirs, we experience profound purpose.

⇌

CHAPTER NINETEEN

It's JUST an Indicator!

When we blow it, catch ourselves wallowing in misery, basking in blame, or are just plain ornery and grumpy, it's a signal. It's an indication we've "lost it" for a minute… or two… or a few years. This happens. We're human. The good news is we finally Caught it! The better news is we know how to clean up our mess, learn from our mistake, and do better.

Here's a BIG mistake we make regarding mis-takes! Say we lose a client, botch up a deal, get in a nasty argument, have an ugly divorce, betray someone we love – or a fellow driver, miss an appointment, act like jerks with our children, perform poorly, or ruin Thanksgiving dinner. What makes things worse is when we add to our turmoil by building our blunder into a grueling horror movie. One that never ends! We story tell about the pain and distress, reiterate it to anyone who will listen, mull it over repeatedly in our own minds, and add to the fiasco by not taking responsibility for our ideas, feelings, and sensations regarding the upset. Or… we don't say a word about it, pretend it isn't under-coating our life, and live in our resistance to the drama until we explode or become ill with disappointment. If we stay in our sad, grumpy, mean vibration and don't apply Catch & Release we multiply the mess.

The quicker we own what we are feeling and release it, the sooner we can access intuition and discover the solution for taking right action. Releasing the nagging sensation or emotion leads to knowing what to do next. The mistake can easily be remedied in this way. Clarity and relief follow. When we have a bad feeling, it is an indication that something is out of whack! IT'S AN INDICATION! It's a good thing!

I love this story from Esther Hicks of Abraham-Hicks:

"You guys get an indication that your vibration has dropped, you get a physical indicator, maybe something to do with your body or a relationship and you make such a big deal out of it. It's just an indicator your vibration is off! You make the indicator something so much more emphatic than it is. You say, "Oh no, look what I have come to!" We say, "No, look where you temporarily are, it's just an indicator." And you say, OH, BUT LOOK WHAT HAS HAPPENED TO MEEEE!! We say, "It's just an indication that your vibration is off, it's just an indicator to offer a different vibration. You repeat, "BUT LOOK WHAT I HAVE COME TOOOOO!!!" We say, "Offer a different vibration and you will get a different indicator."

You don't go to the gas station, just barely limp in, your gas gauge on empty, and just sit there in a heap of depression all day thinking, "Oh look what I have come to... I am on empty... I thought I would do so much better... look what has become of me!"

Abraham repeats, "It's just a stupid indicator, fill up your tank and get on with life you see."

Indicators are our friends. They remind us to pay attention to what we are doing with our attention and energy so we can retrieve it and direct it toward something we prefer to experience!

If you are attracting someone who keep's the horror movie rolling this is a perfect subject to apply Catch & Release to! You might explore for ways this storytelling drama machine is mirroring you? Is there some situation where you do this with others? Explore for how you may keep bad news traveling and growing in certain areas of your life or another's life. For real fun, look for your motivation for doing so and own and release that!

When relationships aren't flowing, when your body is hurting or someone at the office is annoying you in the direction of jumping off of a cliff or the family is at each other's throats, Catch & Release. Let go of any resisted feelings so intuition can show you the way to solution!

If something is driving you crazy… it's an indicator! Empty out the resisted feeling and fill up your tank with something you prefer!

Welcome to Door #19

Appreciating Indicators

•When you are nudged by an indicator practice gratitude for Catching it! Appreciate the indicator for reminding you to collect your creative energy and be free of resistance.

•If you resist indicators, find the feeling(s), idea(s), or sensation(s) you are NOT wanting to have. For example, if you resist not being more together after all this time on earth or more enlightened already, Catch & Release any resistance to this notion so you can allow yourself to be human. Breathe in willingness to allow the ups and downs of the roller coaster ride through life and I bet you get good at putting your hands up on the crazy turns!

≈≈

The Miracle

It is absolutely certain, whether you know it or not,

Or believe it or not,

That every single thing, to the last detail in your life,

Is created by you, desired by you, valued by you,

Clearly, chosen by you.

And in your freedom, when you CHOOSE to let go of fear,

Your life will truly seem to be turned upside down.

And the world will call it a miracle.

Brent Haskell, Ph.D, D.O.
Journey Beyond Words,
A Companion to The Workbook of The Course

≈≈

CHAPTER TWENTY

The Earth Buffet

Do you realize that every single thing you do is because you want to have a feeling? Every action you take is because you would like to cultivate a certain experience. From brushing your teeth in the morning all the way to what time you crawl into bed at night, you do what you do because you want to create a feeling. A feeling you have decided is important to have!

Consider Earth as an enormous buffet of sensations. There you are, cruising the buffet looking for that perfect experience. You know it's there somewhere! You've had a glimpse of it. You've seen others with their plates filled to the brim with this feeling you've been starving for. You keep searching, you nibble on a few experiences that are close to what you are after, but they just aren't satiating. You want that fully satisfied feeling! You continue down this unending display of choices with selections rolling out in front of you as far as your eyes can see! Suddenly, you become very excited! You see an item ahead that draws you toward it like a magnet! "This is it," you claim with heightened anticipation. Your mouth begins watering and your heart is racing. You move closer, shaky with excitement! You've wanted to have this feeling for as long as you can remember. You reach, you're right there. All it takes is scooping some onto your plate. You're ready, mouth watering and…

You look over at the beets and brussel sprouts. You really don't care for beets or brussel sprouts, but you hear a voice inside your head that warns… *"You can't have any dessert unless you eat all your vegetables!"* Your shoulders slump instantly as you surrender to that voice that sounds an awful lot like your mother. You find yourself retracting your arm, retracting your dream, and turning toward what you 'should' do. Mechanically repeating the instruction, "I should probably do the veggies first."

What feeling have you been hungry to experience for a long time, but haven't been allowing yourself to have because there is something you need to do first? Really, what is your 'food' of choice? Would you like to feel some satisfaction, joy, love, hope, connection, appreciation, or something else? And dear friend, what has to happen before you can let yourself enjoy the sensation you are eager to experience? What are you always reaching for when you stand in front of the Earth Buffet? Do you go for the same food repeatedly without giving yourself a broader choice?

What rules have you made regarding being happy or satisfied? What has to happen first? What needs to smooth out at home? What needs to change at work? Who do you need to spend more time with? What has to happen with your body? What would you like to own that might bring you the feeling of accomplishment you long for? Who has to be in your life for you to allow yourself to have a feeling you want to exist? Do you have to struggle sufficiently first so you don't feel guilty for feeling good right now? Where have you drawn the finish line that needs to be crossed so you can enjoy this moment of existence? The one right here, right now?

Do you ever hear yourself say, "When I get this client or have this relationship or when I feel better and get this done, *then* I'll be happy, *then* I'll be okay!" As though happiness is a reward you'll give yourself once you reach some experience or time in the future? Have you ever noticed this pool of joy you plan to jump in later rarely has enough water in it?

We have it backward. By reserving our happiness or satisfaction for later, we miss the magic this vibration of peace, appreciation, or excitement can attract into our lives RIGHT NOW! This is the secret to manifesting a life you love to live! Don't wait to enjoy the profundity of your existence, don't miss the joy of your journey! Don't skip looking deeply into the eyes of your beloved and letting that fill you to the core, every single day! Don't forget to see the magic all around you, in the waving trees, the vast blue sky, in your family's smiles and in your own eyes. It's there inside of you, surrounding you and embracing you... waiting for you to remember.

You have always had the ability to pick your feeling from the buffet and cultivate it so you can attract dreams into your world! Remember when you were a child when you would play, you did it spontaneously, easily, and naturally. Inventing, feeling, imagining, and enjoying each day to the fullest. You truly are a weaver of reality. You get to decide.

When you are ready, select a feeling from the Earth Buffet you are hungry for... perhaps a little satisfaction, accomplishment, or a heap of heartfelt appreciation to view life through. Look any resistances you have to letting life love you right now, straight in the eye, and apply Catch & Release. They are just old thoughts and ideas you have been swallowing for a long time. Let go of fear and open the door to dreams. It is from this place and through these kind eyes that the most intuitive and efficient path to your goals will be revealed. The joy you have scheduled for the future can begin now.

Happiness is a choice not a reward.

≈≈

The most valuable skill or talent that you could ever develop is that of directing your thoughts toward what you want to be adept at quickly evaluating all situations and then quickly coming to the conclusion of what you most want—and then giving your undivided attention to that. There is tremendous skill in deliberately directing your own thoughts that will yield results that cannot be compared with results that mere action can provide.

Abraham by Esther and Jerry Hicks

≈≈

What do you want? What is enjoyable, fun, enlivening, and rewarding? It is such a profound question to answer authentically from your heart with passion. Contemplate, explore, and feel... what do you want? There is a dream waiting for you to remember it.

> *The real questions are, what do you treasure, and how much do you treasure it? Once you have learned to consider these questions and to bring them into all your actions, you will have little difficulty in clarifying the means.*
>
> A Course in Miracles, Marianne Williamson,
> Gerald Jampolsky, M.D., and Kenneth Wapnik

❧

You create abundance from feeling excitement! You create the perfect relationship from being authentically you! You create a healthy body from putting more attention on what you want than you are putting on what you don't want. You will manifest dreams of any caliber from being passionate! Yes, this moment right now, right here, is the one you get to decide in!

Enjoy the path you're choosing to travel. This is the mark of a successful life. Allow the bumps, climb the mountains, apply Catch & Release to resistance along the way, and smile frequently at your friend in the mirror. Be kind to yourself as you learn to negotiate the turns and integrate unexpected stops. Get good at filling yourself up after each flat tire. Being happy all the time is not the goal, owning how you feel is! Freedom is a result of taking responsibility for your choices, without blame of self or another!

Please remember one thing along the way… YOU are pretty darn amazing! You have to admit, you are determined like a bull, you never give up on being a better person, and you love learning how to be more effective at *everything!* Have fun learning, becoming, and growing... enjoy your journey. Get good at having the feeling you want for your first course, as often as possible!

There is a chance we'll arrive at the end of our road sooner than we anticipate, it happens. Don't get there and say, "Oops, I missed dessert and didn't enjoy my life the way I had always planned to." **Decide now,** to feel tremendous gratitude for your time on Earth. Acknowledge yourself for all those mountains you've already climbed. **Decide now,** to look back and smile at where you have been, appreciating the joy you have felt and shared with others. **Decide now,** to acknowledge yourself for how you encourage those near you, inspiring and reminding at every turn. **Decide now,** to feel thankful for how deeply you have been able to love.

And... when you reach that fork in the road that takes you from this precious life to what is next, you will look back on your travels with loving eyes, a full heart, and a feeling of gratitude for every single moment.

It's a good day to smell some roses!

Endless love,

Holly

⌒⌒

Sometimes I believe in as many as six impossible things before breakfast!

Alice in Wonderland

Resources

Audio Programs

Abraham by Esther and Jerry Hicks – *The Law of Attraction*

Abraham by Esther and Jerry Hicks – *The Art of Allowing*

Abraham by Esther and Jerry Hicks – *Ask and It Is Given*

Eckhart Tolle – *Findhorn Retreat: Stillness Amidst the World*

Eckhart Tolle – *Living a Life of Inner Peace*

Eckhart Tolle – *The Power of Now*

Gregg Braden – *Speaking the Lost Language of God*

The Movie Leap! – *www.LeapMovie.com*

The Living Matrix – *www.TheLivingMatrixMovie.com*

References

Braden, Gregg, 2005. *The God Code: The Secret of our Past, the Promise of our Future.* Carlsbad CA: Hay House.

Campbell, Kayt, 2011. *Me, not Me – Living the Difference Between Who We Are and What We're Not.* Joy Publications.

Chopra, Deepak, 2009. *Reinventing the Body, Resurrecting the Soul,* New York: Harmony Books.

Gurdjieff, G.I., 1963. *Meetings with Remarkable Men (All and Everything),* London: Penguin Press.

Gurdjieff, G.I., 1973. *Views from the Real World, Early Talks of Gurdjieff,* New York: Dutton.

Haskell, Brent, Ph.D., D.O., 1994. *Journey Beyond Words: A Companion to the Workbook of the Course in Miracles,* Los Angeles: DeVorss & Company.

Harding, Douglas E., 2005. *Open To The Source: A Practical Guide for Seeing Who You Really Are.* Carlsbad, CA: Inner Directions Publishing.

Hawkins, David R., 1995. *Power vs. Force.* Carlsbad, CA: Hay House.

Hicks, Esther and Jerry, 2004. *Ask and It Is Given: Learning to Manifest Your Desires.* Carlsbad, CA: Hay House.

Hicks, Esther and Jerry, 2009. *The Vortex: Where the Law of Attraction Assembles All Cooperative Relationships,* Carlsbad, CA: Hay House.

Hoff, Benjamin, 1998. *The Tao of Pooh.* London: Mandarin Publishing.

Katie, Byron, and Stephen Mitchell. 2007. *A Thousand Names for Joy: How to Live in Harmony with the Way Things Are.* New York: Harmony Books.

Katie, Byron, and Stephen Mitchell, 2003. *Loving What Is: Four Questions That Can Change Your Life.* New York: Three Rivers Press.

Katie, Byron, and Michael Katz, 2005. *I Need Your Love— Is That True?* New York: Three Rivers Press.

Kennedy, Kayt, 1999. *Love Precious Humanity: The Collected Wisdom of Harry Palmer.* Altamonte Springs, FL: Star's Edge International.

Ouspensky, P.D., 1971. *The Fourth Way.* London; Vintage Books.

Nicoll, Maurice, 1984. *Psychological Commentaries on the Teaching of Gurdjieff.*

Osho, 1977. *The Path of the Mystic.* Pasadena, CA: Theosophical University Press.

Osho, 2004. Freedom: *The Courage to Be Yourself.* St. Martin's Press.

Palmer, Harry, 1994. *Living Deliberately: The Discovery and Development of Avatar.* Altamonte Springs, FL: Star's Edge International.

Palmer, Harry, 1994. *ReSurfacing: Techniques For Exploring Consciousness.* Altamonte Springs, FL: Star's Edge International.

Renard, Gary, 2006. *Your Immortal Reality: How to Break the Cycle of Birth and Death.* Carlsbad, CA: Hay House.

Robbins, Mike, and Richard Carlson, 2007. *Focus on the Good Stuff: The Power of Appreciation.* San Francisco: Jossey-Bass.

Roberts, Jane, 1969. *Seth Speaks.* San Rafael, CA: Amber-Allen Publishing. Upper Saddle River, NJ: Prentice Hall Trade.

Russell, Bertrand, 1997. *Principles of Social Reconstruction.* 2nd Ed., London: Routledge.

Schucman, Helen, 1976. *A Course In Miracles.* Mill Valley, CA: Foundation for Inner Peace.

Tolle, Eckhart, 2005. *A New Earth: Awakening to Your Life's Purpose.* New York: Dutton.

Tolle, Eckhart, 1999. *The Power of Now: A Guide to Spiritual Enlightenment.* Vancouver, Canada: Namaste Publishing.

Tolle, Eckhart, 2003. *Stillness Speaks,* Vancouver, Canada: Namaste Publishing.

Williamson, Marianne, 1992. *A Return to Love.* New York: HarperCollins.

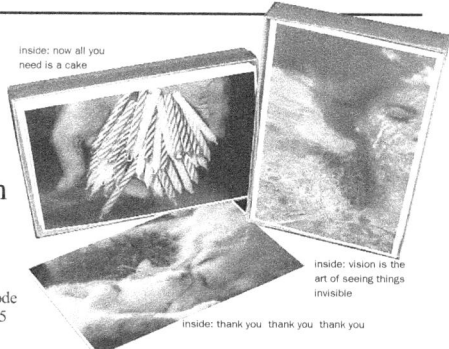

211